BEYOND RECOVERY
Nonduality and the Twelve Steps

Fred Davis

NON-DUALITY PRESS

BEYOND RECOVERY

First English edition published December 2012 by NON-DUALITY PRESS

© Fred Davis 2012
© Non-Duality Press 2012

NON-DUALITY PRESS | PO Box 2228 | Salisbury | SP2 2GZ
United Kingdom

ISBN: 978-1-908664-27-3

www.non-dualitypress.org

Disclaimer: Beyond Recovery and any associated websites or materials are for educational purposes only and are not intended in any way to be a replacement, or a substitute for, qualified medical, psychological or addiction advice, diagnosis, treatment or therapy from a fully qualified source. If you think you are suffering from a medical, psychological or addictive condition, consult your doctor or other appropriately qualified professional person or service.

DEDICATION

This book is dedicated to my beloved wife and
guardian angel, Betsy Hackett-Davis, from whom
I learned about Presence first-hand.

Thank you for everything, my love.
You are my very own Heart.

CONTENTS
and CHAPTER SYNOPSES

CHAPTER ONE—Honesty • 1
Step introduction. Real power is found in surrender. Different levels of surrender. Bondage *to* self. Reality vs. story. The Way of Large Numbers. Mind as a tool to transcend itself. The 180 paradox. Bodies seen as suits. The spiraling way of wants. Denial of overall powerlessness. Using suffering as a signal. Entity equals suffering.

CHAPTER TWO—Conviction • 16
Step introduction. Nondual decision is not our own. Goal of Nonduality. Nonduality encompasses *everything*. Everyday life with a new twist. The voice in our heads. Personal identity is a moment to moment illusion. The Zone. The painful insanity of an exclusive identity. Post-addictive "ism" of addiction seen as insanity. **Exercise 1: A Sense of Being.** *What is* rules.

CHAPTER THREE—Surrender • 30
Review of steps one and two. Step introduction. Our core addiction. Free will versus destiny. The way duality works. Layers of ignorance. Truth vs. ignorance. Tending to the dream. Prayer and *what is*. Where we take our stand dictates our reality. Enlightenment is not a drug. The strawberry story. Surrender is always right now. Freedom and restriction. Fear and war. What we're really afraid of. Opinions vs. reality. Rehearsing war. Reality is simple. What "should be" vs. what is. Verbness of life. Awakening is a story, too.

Amends and arrest. Fred's awakening stories. The witness state. The enlightened ego. The (sometimes) practice trap. The (sometimes) study trap. Spiritual experiences come and go. Nonduality is practical. Enlightened action. How things should be. We are not the boss of *what is*. All the decisions we don't make. We can't really surrender so long as there's someone to do it. **Exercise 2: Noticing What We Don't Notice. Exercise 3: Where's Fred?** The question that has no answer.

Step introduction. Embodying enlightenment. Some thoughts about spiritual teachers. Finding the light through following the dark. Beyond "defects of character." Clarity often comes with distance. Investigating impersonal patterns. The difference between an activity and an entity. Staying awake to confusion. Surrender is allowing things to be as they are. Instructions on taking the Nondual fourth step. **Exercise 4: The Photographer.** Fredness vs. Fred.

Step introduction. Bring clarity to confusion. Our goal is discovering the truth. Letting ourselves off the hook. Transcending the boundaries of illusion. **Exercise 5: A Way of Seeing.** Who wakes up? Waking up is simply a *recognition*. Humanity and divinity. Opening 360 degrees. The dictionary path. This is it.

Step introduction. Employing different systems of understanding for different systems of understanding. Living truth means staying open to new truth. Uncertainty is part of reality. Having it all "right" vs. having it all. Patterns change to fit what is seen. What is seen changes when our stand is taken in awareness. Points of view are owner free. Willingness to be as we are until we're not. Buddha and the poisoned arrow story. Reality as the body tells it. Mind superimposes story and personalization onto reality. The primary tradeoff in life. Dying to reality.

spiritual emergency room. We are God's will. *What is* is God's will. Even surrender is a story. The left hand story. Identity disappears between thoughts. It's all just *happening*. Addiction and recovery are yin and yang. A New Zealander's story. The body as junction box. Life itself has no opposite. *Look for what's looking.* Consciousness is not contained in the body-mind. "Waking up" happens out of time. Our inner teacher. **Exercise 9: Meditation and the Inner Teacher**. Consciously abiding in the one thing going on.

Step introduction. How sharing the central message of freedom is changing for both recovery and Nonduality. Recovery treatment centers, halfway houses and professional counseling. *The Power of Now*, Oprah, the internet and the Nondual boom. Money and the spread of Nonduality. Enlightenment is nothing personal. Trading in being a taker for being a giver. The Zen Ox-herding Pictures. Stabilization and clarity. Returning to the world to offer help. Service is a hallmark. No one is asleep; no one wakes up. "Chosen ones." The long, strange dream. Boundless possibilities.

FOREWORD

FRED DAVIS IS WELL QUALIFIED TO WRITE A BOOK ABOUT NONDUALITY and recovery from addiction for two reasons—he spent many years in recovery himself and has a deep and interest in, and love of, the nondual understanding. In *Beyond Recovery*, Fred takes the approach that characterises the Twelve Step Programme originally designed for recovering alcoholics, expanding and infusing it with his understanding of the non-dual perspective that lies at the heart of all the great religious and spiritual traditions.

However, this is not just a book for recovering addicts, unless we are willing to admit that the vast majority of humanity are addicts without realising it. Let us provisionally define addiction as any compulsive behaviour that is designed to alleviate the pain inherent in believing ourselves to be a limited fragment, separate from the totality. In this case, most of us are addicts to compulsive thinking—if not to substances or physical activities. This does not turn an individual into an addict as such, but exposes conditioned and chronic patterns of thinking, feelings, acting and relating that dominate the life of an individual, obscuring and colouring the natural and effortless ease that lies in the simple acknowledging of experience as it is.

It would not do *Beyond Recovery* justice to reduce it to a programme of steps designed to expose and relieve the suffering that is inherent in our contraction around an imaginary separate self, a sort of personal centre to the universe around whom all experience is believed to revolve. Its real quality lies in the honest, humorous and warm-hearted ways in which Fred explores and exposes the complex patterns of avoidance and denial that characterise the resisting, seeking self and the non-judgmental way in which he describes it. Drawing on numerous examples from his own colourful life, he speaks with passion and humility of a path that started for him as an obsessive search for happiness in the acquisition of objects, relationships and states, evolved through addiction, recovery, spiritual seeking and self-enquiry, and continues in an ever-deepening surrender to the undeniable, unnamable reality of what eternally is.

If the true measure of a book is to be found in the perfume that remains behind when all the words have been forgotten then, for *Beyond Recovery*, it is this quality of honesty, openness and surrender which communicates itself in the words and between them, administering not just to the mind but to the background of Awareness.

Rupert Spira
Oxford, September 2012
www.non-duality.rupertspira.com

INTRODUCTION

There is just one thing going on

Everything—you, me, the earth and the sky, the flowers and trees, mountains and seas, and all that walks, swims, or flies— constitute just a single, integrally connected, flowing *oneness*. It is always moving, always morphing, always reshaping itself through endless changes. And the greatest change in history is happening right now, in our lifetimes.

We've heard people casually state that "we're all one," and related statements many, many times. The *concept* of oneness, while it remains merely a concept, is hardly a radical notion. Yet when this idea of oneness moves beyond the conceptual, beyond ideas, and into *actual, lived experience*, then this "notion" becomes absolutely revolutionary; totally transformative on both a personal and a planetary level. There appears to be just such a revolution happening in our world. Given that you've come to be reading this sentence, there's a strong likelihood that it's specifically happening within you as well. The universe, shall we say, is waking up to itself. It is consciously waking up to both the fact of, and the knowing experience of, its own being and its own singularity.

The universe itself is *alive*; everything that *is* is one living *beingness*.

There is just one thing going on.

The wisest of the wise, East and West, have known the nature of this beingness for several thousand years. Throughout history men and women have left their villages, homes, and families to travel to distant deserts, mountains and jungles seeking a monastery or hermitage, or the proverbial old man on the mountain, where they might find an unveiling of the truth that is reflected in that single declaration of a living oneness. Fortunately we don't have to do that, but some of that same courage and earnestness will go a long way in helping us discover that truth for ourselves—and to actually begin to *live* it. That's what we have come here to do.

A spiritual quickening

People all over the world are "waking up" to their true nature, to their true relation to this beingness. Something like a spiritual "quickening" has gained momentum over the past two centuries, especially in the last fifty years, and dramatically in the last fifteen, since the advent of the internet. That integral connectivity suddenly had a medium through which to connect with itself globally as easily as it could locally. In physics it is known that when momentum's mass grows, so does its velocity. This awakening movement is growing larger and faster, and then larger and faster again, and it is changing both our world view, and our world, as it does so.

Not just for the elite

Enlightenment is not a delusion or a fairy tale. It's not just for the spiritual elite, or the lucky few. It's real, and to a great degree, a methodology for reaching it can be *taught*. Granted, the receiver has to be ready for such a transmission; there are never any guarantees. But if the right degree of earnestness is present, then the truth of our being is bound to be discovered. A dedicated spiritual seeker now has a wonderful chance of becoming a real live spiritual *finder*. Be clear that what I'm saying is that *you* can almost surely wake up if you want to *badly enough*.

Nonduality means oneness

Nonduality is the term we use to label the exploration of this oneness. It directs us toward recognizing our inherent oneness for our very own selves. "Non" means "no" and "duality" means "more than one," so this is the philosophy of not-more-than-one. The effectiveness of this teaching is *measurable*. We change, or we don't; we can judge it for ourselves. We wake up, and/or we see others wake up, or we don't. Again, we ourselves are the judges. I know of no other spiritual teaching whose success or failure is so clear, evident and public. You're surely going to be hearing more and more about it in coming years as this teaching quietly spreads like an ocean of dye as it makes its way around the globe. Wherever it goes there is marked change.

Even if you have never heard of Nonduality, it doesn't matter. That might even work *for* you, simply because you won't have to unlearn or overcome a bunch of intellectual knowledge. Such knowledge can be very helpful, but if we don't stand *upon* it and reach *beyond* it, then it can become a hindrance. I have seen two men, neither of whom knew anything at all about this teaching, come to an awakening as we were going through some investigation together. They didn't need background. Just like in recovery, they needed honesty, openness, willingness and, in their cases, trusted guidance. It's the principles themselves that are important. In reading this book you'll feel a strong pull if this is your path. If it is your path, it can't be avoided.

My own spiritual journey began decades prior to my entering recovery, but until I became abstinent there was no consistency in my study or practice, and no quietness of mind, circumstances that are extremely helpful in "encouraging" grace, we could say. I did get a clear glimpse of my true nature fifteen years before a larger awakening occurred, but that ended up haunting me more than aiding me. After that experience I spent my days loaded and goaded, until I was driven to give up my addictions and returned, in my case, to the lonely path of truth.

I'd had a taste. Once I was clean and sober and reasonably sane and stable, I wanted more of what I'd seen those years ago. The image of that experience never faded one bit. So it was through recovery, and through my working the Twelve Steps, that I gained enough physical stability and presence of mind to chase enlightenment in an orderly and sustained fashion. While it may be completely unnecessary for someone else, in my case all of that sustained chasing was apparently exactly what I needed. *Something* worked.

Nonduality and recovery

I've always been struck by the similarities between the process of getting clean and sober, and the process of spiritual awakening. So I want to share the view from "this side" with those who appear to be on "that side" in the same way that I shared the message of freedom-through-recovery with thousands of alcoholics and addicts over the years. Sadly, in the very same way it was with Twelve Stepping, I can share this until I'm blue in the face, and use the sharpest, clearest language available, but my eager victim who's heart is screaming for enlightenment simply will not, cannot wake up until it's their time to do so. That's the way of it. Nonetheless, having had a number of people awaken while we have been talking about this, I do know that what I present here is effective in helping others. This is not mere theory; it is *field proven*.

I'm eternally grateful to my old Twelve Step fellowship, which is why I never name it. They prefer anonymity, and that's fine with me. They saved my life, and they gave me the stability and mindfulness I needed to get back on the spiritual path. It was my gratitude to the Twelve Step community that initially drew me to start writing this book in my head; I've been thinking about it for two or three years, and then suddenly everything fell together and here it fell out of my head and onto paper. It is an offering to all of you out there, in or out of a fellowship, in or out of recovery, who are looking for the *next* step in your spiritual journey. Perhaps this is it.

The Twelve Steps outline a program of action that recovery literature fleshes out, and the fellowships then teach people to live by it. In that same way, the twelve chapters that follow this one will offer a view of a new way of life, and flesh out this beautiful teaching until a firm foundation is poured and set for you to walk on. I present my take on Nonduality, and use the structure of the steps to hang it on.

Enlightenment is the "natural state"

Walking this path to its natural conclusion—*enlightenment*—changes our entire perspective—on everything, *including* our ideas about this strange thing called enlightenment. Our problems are not necessarily solved, but we do find that most of them will lose their charge. They just won't have the same hold over us. Over time we resonate less and less with fear and anger. When fear or anger are experienced they're likely to be quick and sharp, followed by their ever-faster disappearance. Our pressing spiritual questions may not all be answered, but many of the ones that aren't will immediately cease to be so important. The deadly seriousness of everyday life is dramatically lessened, or even eliminated. There is a flood of peace, an experience of freedom and overall well-being that was previously unknown to us. We will *immediately* know things we cannot even dream of until it happens. For the human being apparently experiencing this shift, it's like receiving a high-speed download. Enormous change can take place in seconds.

While in my experience there is an ebb and a flow to the bliss that often accompanies awakening, the underlying peace, freedom, ease and comfort can become our everyday experience. In fact, that's our goal, so to speak. We're not looking for another great buzz; we've seen where that leads. We are seeking a stable shift that requires absolutely no effort to maintain. Some call it the "natural state." That's as good a name as any. As incredible as it may seem, this experience is actually available to every human being at every moment. You don't have to be special to "get it." In fact, our insistence on being special is precisely what keeps us from it! The more ordinary you are, the better. It is the closeness of truth that throws us, not the distance.

For the record, this teaching assumes the reader is already abstinent, thus it does not address how to get that way. If you are experiencing active addiction, seek help through a Twelve Step program,
or other professional care. Sometime down the road, come back and
read this book if you still feel so drawn. If you are already a member
of a Twelve Step fellowship or other recovery method, this book is
not a replacement for that program, but rather a way to augment
it. Finally, this book won't help anyone achieve financial security,
or acquire the mate of their dreams, but neither will it stand in the
way of those things. It's entirely unnecessary for us to renounce
anything in the normal realm of human experience—except the
sanctity of our thinking. A change in how we live or how we
behave might be a side effect, but it's a completely backwards notion
to think they might be some prerequisite. Natural living *follows*
natural being, not the other way around.

We will use the Twelve Steps for the sake of an introductory
structure, but the book is not *about* the Twelve Steps. Let's understand straightaway that this is *not* a standard recovery book. It's
written for sober, abstinent people who are most likely standing
at a spiritual cliff edge. Often these cliff edges coincide with lives
that may be in crisis, or dramatic flux. That's not required, but very
much like recovery, it's a common way this teaching is discovered.
No one arrives in recovery on a roll, and few arrive here in that
condition either.

Nonduality is there to catch us when we jump from the known
into the unknown. This book is designed to be a bridge between
the Twelve Step community and the Nondual community; a bridge
that carries traffic both ways. It has the power to help bring about
a dramatic shift in the lives of the people who closely resonate with
it. It also has the power and purpose to introduce people in Nonduality to the practical miracle of Twelve Step recovery. Teachers
should know about it. Some Nondualists who are not in recovery
probably should be, and this may give you a more comfortable way
of thinking about it.

The Fred story

I don't want to get too far into the Fred story, but some of it will serve to introduce me as a human being, and to illustrate the teaching. That, by the way, is the only reason I'm telling *any* of the Fred story in this book. After all, it's just another *story*.

For a long time, even prior to active, obvious addiction, I was not an especially nice guy. I wasn't an absolutely *terrible* guy, but I was a far cry from being anyone's role model. As age is wont to do, that pattern wound down some as I grew older, but in many ways I still remained self-centered and acted in very selfish ways even well into sobriety. I was *trying* to be less selfish, and to take responsibility for my actions, and I had made some mighty progress, but as addicts we know better than most that old patterns often die long, hard deaths.

I was a quick and funny guy, and thus *generally* liked, but rarely *dearly* liked. In my romantic life I was the kind of guy who was easy to love when I was around, and yet there was not a lot of love lost once I was gone. I've had way too many romantic relationships in my life, and probably a hundred jobs. Stability, as you can see, was never my strength. Stubbornness was. In every area of my life I was all about doing things *my way*, but sadly enough, my way never worked out very well, or not for any length of time. Thus when I was thirty years old I found myself bedding down under heavy medication in the locked facilities of a mental hospital. For the *second* time. This is not a life that's on track for good things to happen.

I was in that mental hospital because I'd already run my life completely into the ground through active addictions to numerous substances and behaviors. What I wanted was a change of state from whichever one I was then experiencing, and I was willing to do damn near anything to get one. I was always on the hunt for any version of reality other than *this* one. Beyond alcoholism and drug addiction, I had a whopper of a gambling problem. That gave rise to big time lying and stealing, and I was good at both. I've used everything from a lock pick to a shotgun to get what I wanted. I overdid everything I could, every time I could, any way I could.

So I had arrived at the mental hospital at a point of critical mass. I was a stone's throw from a life that would be spent in the gutter, a locked ward in a hospital, or a locked cell in a prison. Name your poison, but they were all lousy options. It doesn't even make sense that I avoided that fate. Gratitude has deep roots here. A little background is in order.

I grew up in South Carolina in the 1950's. Ours was an apparently middle-class family that was actually poor as dirt. My father had been a practicing alcoholic for most of his life and as we've already seen in my story—and probably yours—addiction doesn't make for any sort of security, be that financial, physical, mental, emotional, or spiritual. My parents' colorful phrase for financial insecurity was, "The wolf is at the door." Well, the wolf *lived* at our damn door, and even when things began to level out he stayed on my parents' mental porch for the rest of their lives.

I was apparently fine until I started school, where I discovered I wasn't so fine after all. We were living in a great school district thanks to my parents' wisdom and concern, but that put me in class with the kids of the doctors, lawyers and Indian chiefs who ran my hometown. I developed an acute, chronic case of less-than. I only knew two states: I was either *less* than you, which is how I felt most of the time, or I was *more* than you, which I experienced when I was loaded. As we say in the rooms, I was essentially an egomaniac with an inferiority complex. I heard someone in a meeting describe it as feeling like "the piece of shit around which the world revolves." *That*, by God, is dead-on. This roller-coaster self image of mine never once included *parity*.

In response to this inherent sense of lack I became a bad actor in elementary school. And never really stopped. I ran away from home for the first time when I was twelve. I ran away for the last time when I was forty-five. My life went from bad to worse every time I ran, but I just couldn't *not* do it. This is the nature of compulsivity. In true pathological fashion, I could not learn from experience.

A lot of people in recovery have been homeless. You don't have to be an addict to wind up homeless, although it sure helps. Still, anyone at all, through loss of a job, illness, divorce, sheer bad luck, whatever the circumstance, could end up becoming homeless. If you were *really* unlucky, or fate really had it in for you, perhaps you could end up homeless *twice*. I have been homeless *nine times*. My friends, that is not *luck*. That is *skill*. I am *wonderful* at giving my shit up and ending up on the street. Left to my own devices I will always find a way to suffer. I found a trap door in every "bottom" I ever had until the last one.

Let me give you an example. In 1988, almost as if I was living in a parallel universe where Fred's were fairly reasonable people, I was a successful merchant. I had a nice house, a nice wife, and a nice life. Ten years later I woke up to find myself living as a park bum in Mt. Tabor City Park in Portland, Oregon. I was homeless, helpless, penniless, and clueless. I had no future and no hope. And I had done every bit of the damage myself. Even I, the Teflon wonder, couldn't find anyone else to blame. It hadn't been a straight fall from grace, but it was one hell of a steep slide. Years later, when I would tell this down-and-out story to rooms full of drunks and addicts in treatment, I looked for all the world like this perfectly normal little guy, basically like most of their *dads*, with neatly cut silver hair, wearing khakis and a pressed shirt. I had to go to some lengths to even make the extraordinary nature of my story believable. I would tell them the end of my story before I told them the beginning, just to get their attention. It worked.

So long as I had plenty to drink, I simply didn't think the park was all that bad. I mean there were a couple of scary times with gangs, and I was cold as hell at night, but I had to expect privation. After all, the story that I told myself was that I was a clever Zen master getting back to nature and communing with the squirrels. Zen masters didn't need much. Except a lot of booze, apparently. And cigarettes; lots of those, too. Here's the trap door. When the liquor ran out, the real situation began to settle in. Hunger, fear, regret, and a good case of the delirium tremens beat the arrogance and lies out of me in a hurry. I was now *aware* that I was hiding from cars in the bushes, suddenly scared of my shadow, when something suddenly struck me. Incredibly, even unbelievably, I had been in a nearly identical situation *sixteen years before*.

Way back in the late autumn of 1982, I had woken up one morning in the Arizona desert in a nearly *identical* set of circumstances. After sixteen years, all I had really accomplished was that I'd moved my dilemma from one of the driest places in America to one of the wettest. This is what a *circular pattern* looks like.

I'll cut it short and tell you that I got out of the park within a couple of days of deciding to. Six weeks after I got out of the park I drove back through it in a new Miata convertible. I had a woman on my arm, and money in my pocket. I was a *citizen* again! We parked close to my old hideout, where my old sleeping pad was still under the bushes. Rather than being floored with the gravity of my former situation, and gratefully overwhelmed by my amazing deliverance, I turned the whole thing into the story of a lark in the park by the most cunning guy you'd ever want to meet. I made it sound like a plan instead of a train wreck. This was *not* a guy who was learning anything. This was *not* a guy who'd finished drinking.

Three months later I was on the road again, running back to South Carolina, which was where I'd run *from* ten years before. In my head home had become the new Mecca, which is precisely what Oregon had been a decade back. This is what *circular living* looks like. After continuing difficulties, when I saw homelessness looming in my future again, I got back into recovery. I haven't had a drink, or a drug or placed a bet since March 30 of 2000. I did the whole deal, just like they told me to: meetings, literature, sponsor, steps, and service. To my lasting amazement, after a bit of lag time for the existing fires to burn down, my life even began to improve. You know the rest of the story. It's not so different from yours.

And that's quite enough of the Fred story.

A different kind of awakening

I want to touch on one more thing in this introduction. The spiritual awakening spoken of in this book is not the same awakening typically spoken of in most spiritual or religious circles, or in recovery. This will become apparent as we advance through the book. Enlightenment occurs in all of those traditions, but it's uncommon. Nondual awareness comes when the illusion of separation effectively surrenders to the truth of unity. The difference between the relative surrender of a drop apparently surrendering to the ocean, and the ocean recognizing that no drops exist, is quite significant. It is also experiential. Once you pop the bubble, so to speak, you come to know another level of reality. We may cover it up, but there's no unknowing it. It's very common for our ongoing life patterns to continue to run for quite a while, and we may feel like we're going back and forth between the levels for a quite a while, but what's done is done.

Nonduality and recovery: parallel, not opposing

I was taught when I entered recovery to dwell on the commonalities I would find in other members, and not the differences. It was good advice, and I'd like to air it here as well. Nonduality and recovery don't have to conflict. In physics, for example, classical mechanics describe the way the universe works under certain circumstances, and that's been proven to be a true model. Quantum mechanics describe how the universe works under *another* set of circumstances, and it, too, has been proven to be a true model. Neither model eliminates the need, essential validity, or effectiveness of the other. Recovery and Nonduality could be said to be much the same way. What works in recovery works in recovery. What works in Nonduality works in Nonduality. We could say our goal and approach determine our outcome; neither conflicts with the other. We can embrace both.

This book is for people who are looking for a deeper spirituality than they've yet encountered; perhaps deeper than they imagined was possible. You don't have to change whatever practice you currently do, or your association with any religion or tradition you currently belong to. You can use this book to simply *augment* your current practice or tradition. I invite you to hold onto your current structure; there's neither a right way, nor a wrong way to practice Nonduality, although there are certainly ways that are more skillful than others. But stay in recovery, remain with your church, mosque, temple or synagogue; continue your prayer, meditation, hatha yoga, step work, or whatever practice you subscribe to; all that's fine. Here we are *for* something, but we are *against* nothing. This book can help you take all of that to another level, and gain greater satisfaction and insight from it.

The invitation

For all of the doubting Thomases out there of every stripe, let me offer a famous quote from Herbert Spencer that many of us in recovery will be familiar with. "There is a principle which is a bar against all information, which is proof against all arguments and which cannot fail to keep a man in everlasting ignorance—that principle is contempt prior to investigation." That kind of thinking was nearly the ruination of every addict. Why let it keep us from liberation now?

So, what is Nonduality really all about? We'll explore the answer to that question and many, many more in the next twelve chapters. This might be just what you've been looking for, even if you didn't know you were looking. If so, let me welcome you Home.

CHAPTER ONE
Step One

HONESTY

THE HONESTY TO WHICH THIS STEP REFERS MEANS TELLING OURSELVES the truth about ourselves. In recovery, that truth is about our active addiction. In Nonduality, that truth is about seeing our secret addiction. The solution to both addictions is the same, but neither can begin until the foundation of personal failure has been laid. Our only shot at power lies in accepting our complete lack of it.

That's such a radical idea. On the face of it, it doesn't even make any sense. Yet it's the single most important principle that recovery was founded upon. It's also the principle that underlies all of Nonduality, although it's seen in a very different way. We'll take a look first at this concept through the eyes of the recovery tradition, and then we'll compare that to how it's seen in the Nondual tradition. We'll start with the familiar and then move toward the new.

In the recovery tradition it's always a major hurdle for us to get to the point where we accept our powerlessness over whatever it is that's eating up our lives. We just don't *want* to be powerless, not in anything, not in any way. But in the end we either have to confess it, or go on destroying ourselves.

Let's be candid. Wherever we find surrender in the world, which isn't on every corner to start with, we will find two camps. The large camp surrenders selectively. We surrender to this, but not that. We accept that thing, but not this thing; let go of one event, but not of another. In recovery this selective surrender plays out when we accept our powerlessness over our drug or behavior of choice, but retain the story of our power in everything else. Our life's lack of manageability—which the second half of the first step addresses—is generally seen to be chiefly a symptom of our addiction. We may not say it out loud, but we say it in how we really live our lives. We may do everything else recovery requires of us, but that absolute surrender-to-God's-will thing? Not so much.

There is a small surrender camp where people let go of much more. We often hear from this other camp in the rooms. They tell us to make our best efforts, but leave the results to our Higher Power. That's Nondual wisdom wearing a recovery hat. A lot of people say this, but most of them will then worry about their problems at night. That's not letting go, that's wishing *we could* let go. There are some people, however, who *really* let go. They know that they can't tell a blessing from a curse. They know that those definitions are built around timing. Addiction, for instance, was the worst thing that ever happened to us until it became the best. Without it, most of us would never have taken a spiritual path in this life, and found what we've found. Becoming addicted, in a bizarre way, is the greatest thing most of us ever did. (Or we could say it's the greatest thing we *never* did!) What a great gift!

It's easy to spot members of the small surrender camp within recovery. They're the happiest people in the rooms. They have their share of ups and downs, some days when they behave better than others, and of course they face the same challenges in life that everyone else does. But there will not be any underlying sense of their being "irritable, restless, or discontent." When things don't go their way, they accept and adjust quickly. They will not be consistently reporting anger, fear, resentment, or poor behavior, because even though all of those things may pop out from time to time, they will be far from that person's norm. Surrender isn't something we talk about at this level, it's something that is lived.

If we happen to stumble upon Nonduality, then we will discover a third camp, the smallest of all. In this camp we not only give up our attachments to conditions and outcomes, but we actually give up *ourselves*, or at least the story of ourselves. We trade in our limited identity for an unlimited one. It's not that we merge into the one. There would have to be two in order for a merging to take place. In this third camp it is clearly seen that there is only *one* thing going on to begin with. That thing is *us*. The goal of seekers here, all of their study and practice of this wisdom tradition, is directed toward joining this third camp of absolute, unconditional surrender.

In Nonduality we learn that we've been suffering from another addiction, a secret addiction. We've been suffering from the addiction to self. Rather than merely being caught in the bondage *of* self, we find that we have been caught in the bondage *to* a self. We'll look at this very closely in the third step, but we need to get a feel for it right away.

There is just one thing going on. Our secret addiction, our bondage to a self, is our conceptual resistance to the living reality of oneness. We hang onto this resistance because we don't know any better. We don't know any better, in part, because we *don't want* to know any better. This addiction to self is just like our more obvious one: we aren't going to give it up easily. To overcome it, we have to come to want liberation more than we want anything else, even before we're sure that there is, as Gertrude Stein said, "a there *there*." I'm not so much talking faith as I am intuition, and in some cases a measure of temporary, conditional trust.

The good news about our coming to Nonduality is that we will regularly encounter people who, precisely like the situation in recovery, *have* been there, and *can* point us toward it. In fact, some teachers *knowingly* live in truth all the time. Or we could say they consciously live *as* truth all the time, which is more accurate. Others rely on memory in the same way that clergy rely on holy books, but I say that as an observation and not a criticism. Everyone is right where they're supposed to be, and doing just what they're supposed to be doing; we can bank on that. We can *always* bank on reality! Reality is *what is*. Anything else is simply a story occurring *within* reality. There is no such thing as *what isn't*. We'll say this time and again in an attempt to seep through the mind's defenses.

What we want to do at this stage is begin to open, to allow new ideas to enter, try out suggestions, and then test the evidence as we move down the path. Is this Nondual teaching *working*—for *us*? Are we beginning to see the world in a *distinctly* different way? That's all that counts. Everything else stems from that seeing. No "understanding" of Nonduality is actually required. Ever. *I* don't understand it, and I don't know anyone who does, although I know some extraordinarily wise people. We use the mind, but only with the understanding that the mind cannot transcend the mind, not on its own. Einstein told us, "No problem can be solved from the same level of consciousness that created it."

"Sometimes quickly, sometimes slowly," as we say about getting clean and adjusting to our new way of living. In that same way, we *get* Nonduality the way we *get* it; it unfolds as it unfolds. What we're doing here could be called the Way of Large Numbers. It has been tested and seen to be successful. This is a practical path to enlightenment that can be *taught*. It is a way that can be *duplicated*. We again see a parallel with recovery's cookie-cutter model.

I know people who essentially got "struck by lightning" and their addiction fell away; perhaps you do, too. That's great for them, but what about *us*? How do we follow *that* path—walk around a golf course in a thunder storm holding up a steel rod? The Twelve Steps gave us something tangible that we could not only work for *ourselves*, but which we could also pass along to *others*. What we're doing here is setting up the duplication of what's already been successfully achieved, which is the same cookie-cutter model we used in recovery. It worked for us there, and given enough earnestness, it can work for us here as well.

One of the ways we learn who we are is through discovering what we are *not*. It's a process of reduction, like noticing that when all the aggravating sons-of-bitches who were making us drink and drug left the room, we still wanted to drink and drug. We then had to wonder, "Could the problem possibly be *me* and not *them*?" What a concept! In a not-too-dissimilar way, discovering who and what we are via discovering who and what we are *not* may seem backwards, but historically it works pretty well, and by doing it this way the mind develops less resistance to the teaching. Truth sneaks in the back door.

Nonduality is chock full of paradox, because what we're talking about can't really *be* talked about. Words are the best tools we have, but they are poor ones in relation to the task. We are stuck in the very same place that Lao Tzu was 2,500 years ago when he started writing the Tao Te Ching and said,

> *The tao that can be told*
> *is not the eternal Tao.*
> *The name that can be named*
> *is not the eternal Name.*

Lao Tzu knew he had taken on an impossible task and wanted to state that right up front. I'm doing just the same. Lao Tzu then went on to write a whole book about that which cannot be written about, and I'm merrily carrying on in the same manner. I always was a slow learner. As a *provisional* truth we could say that our mind is *part* of this Tao that Lao Tzu was talking about. I think it will make sense to you that the whole can easily hold all of its parts, but that no part can possibly contain the whole. The mind, the part, just can't grasp this teaching. There's just *what is*, which is beyond either *partness* or *wholeness*, but it's unnecessary for us to understand that just now. Part and whole will do.

The mind is the vehicle we'll use to help us take something of a quantum leap in logic, and actually move *beyond* the mind. This book will give you the opportunity to come to know your own true identity—the single *verbness* that *is*. We'll have to use labels and other concepts in order to properly conduct our investigation, but we never want to believe that any of them are true. They'll still work. I don't have to believe that a hammer will do its job. In the *absence* of any beliefs at all a hammer will still nail things quite wonderfully.

This investigation is really important to us, because it explores the possibility that within the ordinary lives we're living today, right here, right now, there may be an entirely different *living experience*. Not a conceptual thing, not something to read and remember, not something to discuss at a juice bar, or over daiquiris, but a whole new way to be and live. What if we are already in the Promised Land and don't know it? Unless we've previously had a glimpse of this truth, we can't even begin to imagine what that means, or what is really and readily available to us—in *this* life, on *this* planet, in *this* time, *without* us having to be anything or anybody other than who we are, and without buying a ticket to Tibet.

What if we didn't need thirty years of prayer and meditation? Is it possible that in some cases such practices could actually impede our way? Could our case be one of them? We're not speaking for everyone in every situation. We're speaking of *us* in *our* situation. What's right for *us*? Is it at least possible that sainthood may be overrated? Is it possible that trying to be other than the way we already are is the perfect method to prevent us from *being* changed? A *willingness* to be "other than the way we are" is quite different from *trying* to be other than how we are. The former is surrender. The latter is resistance with a pretty hat on it. It's still the same old resistance that's tripped us up all our lives, it just looks better—which makes it all that more difficult to let go of. How well did we do efforting away our obvious addiction? Not so hot. Resistance doesn't work any better here with this more subtle issue, with this addiction to being a separate "me."

I confess to having been *around* recovery for a lot longer than twelve years, but most of that time was spent drunk-and-in-charge. Do you remember that? The whole time my life was going down the tubes I was very clear on what the *rest* of the world should be doing! I was an instant expert on whatever popped into my mind. I might have been drunk or in jail, but by God I was still *right*! Recovery taught me that, for me, being right was a fatal malady. I had to first be wrong before my conditions could begin to right themselves.

That's a perfect example of what I call the 180 paradox. We'll talk about this paradox quite a bit more later, but suffice it to say here that every deep spiritual truth I've ever learned showed me that the world works exactly the *opposite* of the way I always thought it did. I spent my whole life looking for a right turn, or a left turn that would take me out of my troubles. I never once thought about taking a *U-turn* until I absolutely, positively *had* to. I didn't want to be *wrong*. I had a whole life invested in my being right, and to repudiate that would repudiate my entire history. I couldn't see that this was exactly what I needed. We can't see what we can't see until we do.

Here is another 180 paradox: we can never see *the most obvious thing* until we can. Then we can see nothing else, and wonder why in the heck it took us so long to see it. Wasn't the need for us to join recovery just like that? I couldn't see it until I was almost dead! The truths exposed in Nonduality are sort of like that, too. We cannot see the most obvious thing until something courted, yet unbidden happens, and then we can see nothing else. Our seeing of it may be momentary, but it's always unmistakable. It doesn't need any outside verification; they call it self-verifying, and that is my experience as well. Our seeing of it, indeed our conscious *being of it*, can also become continuous. It's not like we can fall away from it, or out of it, although it can feel like that's the case.

Surrender in Nonduality is eventually seen to actually be what we *are*, rather than something we *do*. Everything that *is* has *already* been welcomed—by *us*. Otherwise it could not be. We *are* the welcoming of reality. I know this is confusing; it's unnecessary for us to be masters of this just yet. Let the ideas begin to seep in; that's plenty. Let's agree to be plain, open people for this life, and masters in the next.

If we want to know and consciously be this truth, then we can begin to *practice* doing what it does. Let's practice being ourselves! Let's start welcoming reality, *this* reality, *this* here, *this* now, *this* this, exactly as it is. There's nothing conditional in *that*. For the moment, instead of thinking of our bodies as being "us," let's think of our them as being *suits*, something that we're *wearing*, not something we truly *are*. Let's endow our suits with the traditional Buddhist six senses: seeing, hearing, tasting, feeling, smelling and thinking. Now, let's further pretend that reality—*this* reality—is a movie that our suits are watching. We can learn something of absolutely critical importance this way.

When our suits take in the vast panorama of reality, what do they *do* with it? They would do the same thing all computers do with information, which happens to be the same thing our brains do with information. They *process* it. And what does a "process" of any kind need? *Time*. So, in the relative model there is a delay between *perception* and *reception*, and another one between *reception* and *conception*. In other words, although our suits may be experiencing something called the present moment, we, the wearer, are always looking at the *past*.

Now let's just gently notice that our actual situation is precisely like the one described. By the time our brains process what the body has told them, and that information is made into something useable, we are experiencing the past. Reality is always a done deal. Reality is always "in the can" by the time the brain can even experience it. I offer this to you as a tool, and here's how to use it. I ask you, what is the point in our resisting *what is*, when *what is* already *is*? I can hate that my car is black all that I want, but it doesn't affect the color one iota. I get to suffer, but it doesn't change a damn thing.

We can't change it! We can't fix it to suit our whims! We can't correct it! We can't do a damn thing about it! Ohbn well, yes, it's true that we can resent it and suffer, or we can fear it and suffer, but where's the sanity in *that*? We also have the option of seeing the truth. Reality cannot occur any other way than it occurs. Everything is woven together. Think of it as a giant tapestry, a mile high and a mile wide. The only part we can see is what's right in front of us, and the part that we can see is *already done*! The meal is cooked and on the table; there's no point in wishing the timing or ingredients had been different.

There is no wisdom whatsoever in resisting *what is*. Our mind wants to turn it around and around in the futile hope that if it does so long enough and hard enough it can come up with a workable alternative that better suits our conceptual separate me's desires and demands. But it never will. It can't. It's *over*. Our *perceived* reality is always already past. For goodness' sake, let's just get out of the way and let what already is do what it's already doing!

Surely you remember how difficult it was to face our then-active addictions. We didn't want to have them. That didn't change the fact that we *did* have them, but because we wouldn't fess up, we kept doing the same things over and over again expecting a different result. Only when we came clean about our dirt did we have a chance to get better.

Let's talk a little about my story again.

In early recovery, after having spent nearly a lifetime loaded-and-in-charge I went through a brief period of surrender and amiability with the world as it was. When I saw that I'd previously been wrong when I denied my addictions, and confessed this willful wrongness publicly, something opened up, and I began to see that I'd been dead wrong in a *lot* of my thinking. This kind of humility, however brief, left me willing to entertain all sorts of new ideas and insights. As a result, when early sobriety wasn't utter hell, it was a period of great peace. I remember quite a lot of it very fondly, even though I was poor as a rat and scared to death of ending up drunk or homeless or both. I constantly lived about half a step from homelessness, and yet I learned to be content with both my financial insecurity, and my scorched standing in the non-recovery "real world," where I was just another loser.

Of course that stage of surrender didn't last long; it almost never does. Soon enough I began to take back the reins, succumb to the rising sureness of my own beliefs, opinions, and positions; see just how things ought to be, and complain about my lot in life the same way any poor victim like me would. When I first got to the rooms all I wanted was to not suffer so much. Thirty days later all I wanted was to not suffer so much and have a job. A month after I got a job all I wanted was to not suffer so much, have a job—and a girlfriend. And then a car, more money, a dog, nice weather, polite clerks, good drivers, and on and on and on, trying to fill the hole inside of me with stuff that just kept dropping right on through it. No matter what I got, once again it never was quite enough. I began to worry about the future, which is actually a hell of luxury when you've been in the frying pan for as long as I had been, but of course I didn't see that. When I was living in the park, I wasn't worried about my *future*!

I don't think I was really much worse about this than anyone else, but I certainly wasn't any better. I did the best I could. We all do. I tried on humility and gave it a test drive from time to time, but found that it was a little too constricting. You can't be humble and complain at the same time, just as gratitude and fear can't inhabit the same space. But I didn't drink or use or gamble, I did a lot of service, and my conditions slowly improved—they just didn't improve quite as fast as my sense of entitlement did. We could call this the Spiraling Way of Wants. The truth is, so long as I continued to walk that way, I wasn't surrendered, although I claimed to be. The claiming of it, sadly, left no open space for the universe to work. Tell a lie, live a lie.

So I spent several years in recovery in *unconscious* denial of my powerlessness over anything other than my addiction. I had moved from being drunk-and-in-charge to being sober-and-in-charge! It's a neat trick that they don't actively *teach* us in recovery, but if we watch closely there are plenty of people who'll show us the ropes, without our needing any formal coaching. What we learn is how to surrender *just enough* to remain abstinent-and-in-charge. In this mode, we still get to live our life with rants and tirades, with lasting anger and lingering resentments, but we come tell on ourselves regularly in meetings. We pretend that public confession somehow makes everything okay, and many will obligingly chuckle with us, since we're doing the same thing they're doing. But how many years can we continue to act out as assholes, followed by a prompt confession to it in meetings with a headshake and a sheepish grin, before it becomes clear that we may have some *self-awareness* that we didn't use to have, but that there is still no willingness to *actually change*?

The phrase "progress, not perfection" can become a license to do whatever the hell we want. "We are not saints," is another favorite cop-out that wasn't meant to be a license to be bad, which is often the way we use it.

There is a very similar place we can reach in Nonduality too, so I might as well address it here. We can *believe* Nondual teaching and end up suffering badly. Those around us will suffer, too. There's no sort of classic "conversion" scenario in Nonduality. Teachers are not trying to get anyone to *believe* these teachings. They're not even true! They're *pointing* toward truth, but they're *not* true in and of themselves. Just like the action plan of recovery, we want to get busy and try this stuff out, put it to work in our thinking, our living, and in any practices we might have. A zillion people have read recovery literature and gone on to ruin. An awful lot of people read Nondual material, but stay in what I call "spectator" mode. Nonduality is not a spectator sport. We have to get involved.

I know, I know, the mind will tell us, "Well gee, he's saying that I'm only part of the one thing going on, and thus I can't have free will! Heck, I might as well do whatever I want!" I hear variations on this all the time. This is *not* spirituality. *At all.* This is egoism via intellectualism, and it will lead to either hedonism, or nihilism, or both. Leave it alone for now. The interesting thing is that when it's used like this, "what I want" is never what I think is right, but always what I want to do anyway.

The mind can only hurt itself and others when it toys with that kind of loop. It is poison to progress. Try to accept, just for now, that we can't know what we don't know. Let's give doubt free rein in our minds. Let it gnaw at all of our sure thinking. Let it gnaw at our foregone conclusions. Let it gnaw at all of our BOPs—beliefs, opinions, and positions, *especially* our ones about free will or the lack of it.

Just like in recovery, few people begin studying Nonduality because their lives are going just like they want, and they simply want to amp that condition up with a dose of spirituality. There is usually a crisis of note going on in either the foreground, or the background of our lives (or both) before we begin to reach out for something *else*. If we are rich and good-looking and have the life and lover of our dreams, who on earth is looking for a fix for *that*? No, we come because things have gone south on us. We have tried muscling this crisis away, and that didn't work. As recovery folk, we almost surely tried "turning it over," but for some reason this time we didn't get a lot of relief from that, either.

Whether our situation is acute, blazing pain, or a chronic, dull throbbing doesn't matter. We can't go on, and we can't give up, so we're stuck. *We're hung with our own damn lives.* So, if fate has placed us on the road less traveled, we may turn to Nonduality to see if there's not some way to "side-step" our suffering. Can I acquire and use this thing called enlightenment to help me make an end run around this awful story? Please, God, give me an escape hatch!

That's *exactly* what I tried to do. It didn't work. But I had gotten myself hooked anyway, and the teaching wasn't about to let go of me. What I found out is that we can't ever go around anything. The only way *to* something is *through* something else. If I want to be on the other bank, then I have to cross the river. If I want less suffering, I've got to go through the suffering that I have, and allow it to fully discharge. If I want truth, I've got to work my way through the lies.

We can learn to use suffering as a signal. When our so-called lives really begin to be painful, it's a sure sign that we're caught up thinking, worrying, and scheming over *our life*, and we're taking *our life* really seriously. We are lost in our head, living in either an imaginary past, or an imaginary future. We are not living in our body, where everything is always *just so*. Suffering means we've made something up, and have decided to believe it. We are once again lost in denial, only it's over something other than our obvious addictions. It means we've relapsed into our *core* addiction. Our core addiction is shared by, I would guess, very close to seven billion people. Well over ninety-nine percent of the world believe they are separate entities. Every single one of us feels like the center of *the* universe, because we are visually positioned in the center of *our* universe. It's a combined trick pulled by perception and illusion. Ego is the man behind the curtain. Suffering is its fruit.

In short, when we're suffering, it means that we're cheerlessly living in the denial of oneness. I sheepishly confess it still happens to me. It doesn't happen very often, and it doesn't happen for very long, but it does still happen.

When we're *not* in denial of oneness, we can clearly see that there is just *life as it is*. Only. There isn't anything else. There is no room in *life as it is* for "my life." There's just one thing going on. It's not "me over here and oneness over there," which is a normal human feeling, however untrue. "It's all one except the me over here who's watching it be all one." There is recognizable, patterned activity happening where our bodies live, but it's webbed to the activity of the entire universe. There is no separate entity anywhere, ever, except in our heads. This is why there can't be any free will, nor any lack of free will. Who is there to have or not have it? The basic equation of human life is, "entity equals suffering." We'll be seeing this equation restated in many ways, because this is the obvious, but somehow nearly ungraspable, core of the teaching.

This unity has tremendous diversity—unity doesn't mean that everything is the same. Clearly it's not. So when we join these words, diversity and unity, we come up with *unicity*. That's a helpful word for us. Yet even if we could explain oneness—unicity—with words, this still wouldn't be enough. We are not marching toward a new theology. What we come to Nonduality for is the One Taste. We want to know this oneness for *ourselves*, not just hear about it. Other than our using it as a marker for our own journey, who really *cares* what someone else has experienced? Bully for *them*, but what about *us*? Living on second-hand spirituality is like watching someone else eat a meal and then telling ourselves we're not hungry. The hunger is not going to go away until we satisfy *our* hunger. Spirituality works the same way. We have come here, blindly or intentionally, to genuinely discover for ourselves how things really are, how the world really works.

It comes as a surprise to most people that we genuinely *can* know this for ourselves. If I screw up and mention enlightenment in the wrong company, that person will wince, and then smile nervously while looking for a fast way to part company with the kook. Nonetheless, we can know the most basic truth of the universe. We can know what Buddha and Lao Tzu knew, for example, and thereby experience life in a not altogether different way than they did. We really can come to see as Jesus saw, and understand in a whole new way much of what he said. We, like he, are simultaneously one hundred percent human and one hundred percent divine. We become our own clergy. As farfetched as all that might sound, that's what the teachings of Nonduality are all about, and they've been with us for thousands of years. They have quite a track record. Perhaps they really are worth a look.

If you do join us, I can't advise you to share all of this with all of your friends, not as information prior to enlightenment, nor as living truth in post-enlightenment. We think that upon *our* awakening everyone will be able to feel truth, and hear it through us. It won't happen. People who are really open, by which I mean people who are in deep suffering, or near death, or in serious crisis, may very well feel it, and hear it. They don't have much time left, nor any story left that's worth defending, and so truth has a way to slip in under the door, so to speak. People who want to know the truth more than they want anything else will be able to hear us fairly well. If there is a carpet of trust underlying the relationship, that's very beneficial to transmission as well. But the vast majority simply *will not get it*, and they will not get *us*. The price of this understanding is being misunderstood. If you come aboard, you might as well get used to it.

The great thing about addiction recovery is that, in the face of abject failure, something grand and magical happened to us, and it happened through acceptance. Not through resignation, but through real surrender. So we have some inkling, or maybe far more than an inkling, of what all of this next step is all about. Recovery has done us yet another great favor. It has actually *primed us* for Nondual surrender. It has *primed us* for approaching enlightenment. Recovery has given us one new life already, and now we discover that it has readied us for another! Who could imagine that people such as we could come into such great bounty and beauty? Who could imagine such grace as this?

CHAPTER TWO
Step Two

CONVICTION

WHEN I SPEAK HERE OF CONVICTION, I'M REFERRING TO OUR REACHING an unshakable new belief via our own powers of observation and reason. We perform a personal investigation into the nature of our situation, and its result is coming to believe that our old way of seeing things was narrow, inaccurate, and dangerous. Seeing this, we become willing to accept new ideas, which in turn opens us up to more avenues of healing.

One might think, given that initial second step work is done with active addicts, that "coming to believe" in a Higher Power is the more challenging aspect of the step; there's even special literature out there to help people come to grips with it. A great many people arrive at recovery's door claiming to be atheists and agnostics, when in fact their own ego is functioning as the individual's personal god. I've seen it time and again. It's easy for me to see it, because it's how I used to think. We have to put that ego out of the god business, or the person is rarely, if ever, going to recover from their addiction. It's far more important to put the old god out of business than it is to instill a belief in a new one. That's why the language—"power greater than ourselves" is kept so loose.

Recovery is a spiritual program. I used to talk to people sometimes who would say, "I like recovery, I just don't like the spiritual stuff." Whereupon I would ask, "Oh really? Then what *did* you like, the coffee? Recovery is nothing *but* spirituality. We have lousy coffee, a great God, and nothing else. So, if I wanted to recover from my addiction, I'd take a *really close look* at the spiritual thing."

In my experience, however, if the newcomer is sufficiently deflated via his own experience, then coming to an agreement about a Higher Power is not particularly difficult, because no real agreement is necessary. Once it has been conceded by the addict that he or she is in at least deep trouble, and very possibly in mortal decline, and that there appears to be nothing whatsoever they can do about it, the real fight is over. Once we really *see* a lie, we are halfway to seeing *through* it. I found little resistance to the recovery tradition's wide open brand of spirituality once we had framed both the problem and the solution properly. Desperation can do wonders in improving intellectual flexibility.

A similar thing can be said of those of us in the rooms, or from the rooms, who've found our way here to the Nonduality "room." We're average people. Like most people in recovery, the majority of us here no longer have to spend every moment putting out fires (or setting them!) in our everyday lives. We do most of the same things average people do, and have the same things most average people have: a home, groceries, a job, probably a car, perhaps a beloved pet or partner, or both. We have regained, or found for the first time, some measure of peace and self-respect. Some would wonder why then are we even *here*, in search of a deeper spiritual understanding? Who would want to "fix" what's already so good and why? The answer is simple. The decision to come to this teaching is never our own. We come because we have to. We *can't not* come.

For some of us, even when life is quite good, there can still arise an unspecified gnawing, an unfounded *suspicion*, almost, that there is something yet unknown for us, something beyond our current experience. We are drawn to it like moths to a flame. If we are lucky or blessed, before our quest is over we'll go the last few inches and actually *enter* the flame. *Mothness* will die to wholeness. Christians call this sort of thing being "born again." Here I think we could call it being *"unborn"*!

Our spiritual quest can, and often does, become the driving force in our lives, motivated, at least in part, by a relentless curiosity. Nondual teachings use that curiosity as the lever to begin to move Nondual concepts first into our minds, and then, with enough openness and willingness, very rapidly into our actual, everyday, living experience. The goal of Nonduality is the experiential rediscovery of our true nature. This truth has been called many things—enlightenment, liberation, awakening, nirvana, bodhi, "the understanding," freedom, deliverance, "the Way," Divine Union, salvation—the list goes on and on. From the absolute view, coming to this union is our single worthy pursuit in life.

It need not take a lot of time to discover it. If it does, fine, but we want to be clear that it's not *necessary*. (Except for when *it is*.) As an example, I had a phone conversation today with a woman who has been studying Nonduality for twelve years, and had been on a wandering spiritual quest for a couple of decades beyond that. We can agree that this is a *long* time to be pursuing something. She'd read very widely and deeply on the subject of Nonduality. I know of at least one spiritual teacher she'd gone to see—at a group event, not personally—but it speaks of the sincere nature of her investigation. We don't start reaching for help until we first figure out *we can't do it*. That's not easy. In fact, if this "we can't do it" was completely grokked, we could stop our pursuit of enlightenment; it would find us at that very moment.

At the very beginning of our conversation, as soon as my friend had laid this history out, I asked her if she'd yet had an experiential glimpse of her true nature. "Not a thing," she ruefully reported. We began to talk and she woke up in a little over an hour. I didn't wake her up; it's not like that. I do think I provided some assistance in helping her see that she wasn't asleep to being with.

My friend didn't have a fireworks-style awakening, but she came to know the truth of her being, and she *knew* she knew the truth. She knows it *now*, too. We exchanged emails just a couple of days ago. That's *conscious* knowing. That's enlightenment. But let us be clear that glimpsing our *beingness* is the *commencement* of enlightenment; it's not the end of anything but conventional seeking. It is the beginning of a whole new journey that is coming from a whole new place. I have heard that, assuming we remain open to awakeness, it takes five to fifteen years to really settle in. That tallies perfectly with my experience.

Yet Nonduality doesn't simply focus on just the absolute view. It also encompasses respect and joy for the relative environment we all live and breathe in. There is plenty of room here for our families and for our work, for art and sport, for the full range of human activity and emotion. Since there is just one thing going on, then it naturally has to encompass *everything*. We don't have to throw anything out in order to study or follow Nonduality. As it is explained and pointed to here, the Nondual path is all about inclusion, not exclusion. It is the "freedom to be," not "restriction from doing." That may sound like two different ways of saying the same thing, but I assure you it is not.

Everyday life is not made irrelevant, it is simply seen as it is, and thus our experience of it is much lighter and more enjoyable than we previously experienced or imagined. Most things that were important to us prior to enlightenment remain important to us following it. We still love and respect our partners and families—whether they choose this path or not—and we typically still value our homes and jobs, all the normal range of interests. But these things are certainly seen differently, with a new twist, as it were. Regardless, most of the "awake people" I know are incredibly busy, vital people who certainly *appear* to be *doing* a lot of doing right here in *this* world.

When we change the way we look at things, the things we look at change. Our world is our very own private projection. This doesn't mean we make moves to bend the universe. From the Nondual position there is no point in such an exercise. Manifestation, as we hear of it today, is always about an ego striving to improve its dream. *The whole thing is already ours*: what else could we need beyond the everything we already have and are?

From the dualistic view, the world is felt to be *critically* important from a *needy* point of view. We want this, but not that. We desire more of one thing and less of another. We want this experience to extend indefinitely and another to stop right now. This life strategy works for us until it doesn't. Once it doesn't, we are left at least disenchanted, and often depressed. At some point the people who will be drawn to this teaching will discover that the offerings of the world, no matter how luminous and grand, eventually wear thin, or they wear out altogether. If we're not waiting and angling for the world to fill our every demand, every physical, emotional and existential need, then our experience of the world is a lot more enjoyable. It's like letting some of the air out of a balloon. The balloon is still there, but it's not so big, or under so much pressure, and it doesn't require so much of our attention to constantly keep it up in the air.

When we are not so captivated by the objective world, we can experience the pure, transparent and delightful background within which the world occurs. The balloon is left to float on its own, and no longer has to be so heavily watched and guarded. There is more to life than "balloon-ness." We finally get to relax, because we're no longer having to constantly blow our vital forces into it every moment. Amazingly, everything still works, even in the absence of our "help and management." It even works *better*!

Let's explore how this works out in real life. When we read a novel, go see a play, or watch a movie, we get involved. The measure of an entertainment's success is calculated on its ability to get us keenly wrapped up in those characters and their situation. How fast and effectively does it carry us out of this world and into that one? If we encounter weak writing, unconvincing acting, or lousy production values, our belief is not suspended. We'll toss the book aside, or perhaps walk out of the play or movie. Obviously the entertainment failed; it failed to take our attention off of ourselves and our constant whining.

You have a voice inside your head. Check and see if it doesn't spend the great majority of its time complaining. I'm betting it does. It's fussing prior to the entertainment. If we continue to hear that incessant voice during the entertainment, then our hopes for escape from everyday life are dashed; we're again hung with being the same old selves we've been all along. We were promised a dose of a pleasant, if short-lived drug, and we didn't get it. We feel not just disappointed, but deceived.

Conversely, when we *do* get really caught up in an entertainment—books, movies, video games, sports, travel, dining, sex, bird watching, fishing, or what have you—we temporarily drop our current story, and the voice shuts up. Ego makes up an ever-changing story of self that spontaneously arises when our hard-wiring—our DNA—meets inherent conditioning and surrounding circumstances. Nature, nurture, and situation. Our identity is actually a moment-to-moment affair that changes so swiftly it *feels like* there a real core there. There isn't. Like the Invisible Man: it's all clothes and no presence. Hence the incessant voice. In the absence of that voice, there *is no* make-believe separate entity. In the absence of a make-believe entity, there is only *what is*, and *what is* is always peaceful. This can be seen and *lived*, not just dreamed about.

When consciousness is *knowingly* being itself, by which I mean when consciousness temporarily relaxes its identification with a specific body-mind, the apparent resident ego, meaning the loosely aligned series of thoughts, memories and patterns that we think is "us", disappears. This is not a rare occurrence, it's just rare that we *notice* it. If you're not actively reincarnating ego in every fresh second, it disappears. This happens throughout the day, every day, between every single thought. In the absence of ego, truth is seen, but it's not noticed, it's overlooked. Truth doesn't need to be chased, nor does it need to arise. It's already here, all of the time. We can think of ego as being like a rainbow. A rainbow doesn't really exist as a thing, it's just a play of light, but it *appears* to exist from certain vantage points, under certain conditions. In fact, however, a rainbow is not *other than* the sky in which it appears.

This absence of ego—what happens in a movie theater and between every thought—is the same thing that's experienced when we're in the "zone." In the zone, there is a bat hitting a baseball—but there is no one there doing it. That's why the action is so perfect. In the best of art, there is painting, but no artist; writing, but no writer; music, but no musician. We have let go of driving the bus. When people ask, "How do I *learn* to 'let go?'" I point out that they are *already* letting go of everything twice a day: once when they go to sleep, and again when they wake up. Deep sleep is living presence void of identity. It's similar to what an infant experiences: world without label. We *learn* identities, we aren't born with them.

A little later in this chapter we're going to look at some self-inquiry, which is a self-questioning method we can use to check on the validity of our current perception of reality. We're going to look and see if perhaps we're insane. For this moment, a question we might find helpful to ask ourselves is if we are getting beaten up in life because we are experiencing a collision with reality as it is, or if we are being beaten up because our story *about* reality is in collision with reality as it is. An honest look will tell us that we are never being psychologically beaten up by reality, but rather by our failure to *recognize* reality. It's our story of how things *should be* versus things *as they are*. Which side would you guess is going to win that fight—every single time?

One of my favorite sayings is, "In the absence of my opinion, everything seems to be going fine." In the absence of judgment, which can only arise from a seemingly separate identity, there is only *this*. Reality is always simple. It's what's right here, right now, the stuff that a photographer could take a picture of and show to us. Everything else is in our heads, and it's simply *not real*. It's just story; endless, self-perpetuating story.

In full clarity, which means in the recognition that there is no separation of anything from anything else; in the recognition that there is just one thing going on, there is zero psychological suffering. In partial clarity, there is diminished suffering, meaning that the suffering will come and go as clarity comes and goes. We can, however, have an awakening experience, and thus harbor a certain knowledge/memory in our head, and still suffer. I did it for years.

We call that state oscillation, or on-again, off-again enlightenment, or simply "I got it, I lost it!" We suffer in the periods we're
not consciously awake, including *additional* suffering as the result
of having knowledge of a non-suffering condition of which we're
no longer able to partake. You can't miss what you don't know, but
once you know clarity, if you're not consciously in it, you miss it
incredibly keenly. There is another option available. Upon recognizing that we're caught up in mind, we can go into denial, or we can
follow the suffering like a compass toward greater clarity.

In the dream state, in the state where we really believe we are
separate beings, where there's a me over here, and a world over
there, when we are living only *from* ego, and only *for* ego, suffering is the norm. "Life is suffering" is one translation of the
Buddha's First Noble Truth—his very first teaching. Granted we all
have wonderful moments, fabulous periods of great luck and lovely
flow when everything is going our way, but if we look at them at
all closely, we'll see that they come and go. Yin and yang. Up and
down. Ebb and flow. On and off. We're happy during those times,
but not so happy out of them. We have a nutty belief that things
should always go the way our ego thinks they should. This is not
just unlikely; it's impossible. Everything in the dream is balanced.

With all of this as our background, let's now go back to our
Twelve Step model. In working with others in the recovery, whether
it was a single sponsee or a large group in a treatment center, what
I most wanted at this juncture was for them to see that they were
insane. In order for us to be "restored" to sanity, as the second
step's wording indicates, it's first necessary for us to *be insane*, else
we wouldn't need restoration. It always surprises me at how much
resistance there is to this notion. That resistance usually stems from
our having linked our insanity to our addiction. We think our
insanity is caused by our addiction, when in fact it's completely
reversed. Addiction is an effort to deal with the painful insanity
of living in the dream of separation. The "ism" we talk about in
the rooms, when our addiction has been dropped, but life is still a
growling bear, existed prior to our addiction, and remains after our

active addiction is dropped. It's freely acknowledged in the rooms. Another word for that "ism" is insanity.

Until we rediscover our true nature, and recognize the oneness of the world and everything in it *and* out of it, suffering will be a matter of degree and longevity, but it's not going be absent for very long. We may have less of it for a while, and then more of it for a while; it may be present for a long time, or a short time. It may be subtle or overwhelmingly evident. In times of great joy, accomplishment, or acquisition, we may think it's gone entirely, that we've finally figured it all out, and that God is on our side. Tell yourself the truth. How long does that flow usually last? Other than for brief moments, inherent disillusion and dissatisfaction are always either around, or around the corner. "Things are great. *But...*" So long as we are living in misidentification, suffering will remain as the baseline and background of our lives.

Sometimes when we begin to wake up our friends may think we've gone crazy, but the fact is that awakening is the beginning of *going sane*. Enlightenment is not the *end* of the spiritual journey as most of us believe. That's how it's often been sold in the past, but that's simply not true. It is the beginning of a deeper level of spirituality that bears little relationship to the type that is practiced prior to it. Some of the by-products may be the same, such as gratitude, compassion, and generosity, but they'll be coming from a *completely* different view. This is not mumbo jumbo. Awakening is a distinct line, and it is self-affirming. We know the truth when we see it, or more accurately, we know the truth when we *are* it.

Someone who is speaking from awakeness would never declare that they "have it," as if they are personally the proud carrier of something exotic and limited. There is nothing exotic, limited, or static about enlightenment. It's everybody's birthright. We are awake to this ordinary moment, or we are being seduced by the *content* of the moment; one or the other. It's an all or nothing game. We *apparently* grow into clarity within a time frame. Progress beyond the gift of grace, as I see it, comes most often from our willingness to live what we already know; to really allow awakeness to take us over; it flowers when we embrace it, and withers when we ignore it.

Rather than resist either the dissolution of ego, or the continual loss of a constantly rebuilding personal identity, we encourage both. If this sounds scary, let me assure you that we don't really lose a thing. We can't. There's nothing there to lose. The personal identity to which we're so addicted simply *is not real*. The conscious, knowing experience of reality we gain in place of ego—*that* is real. In fact, it is reality itself. Lose nothing and gain everything. Maybe Nonduality is not such a bad deal after all!

Awakening, as I speak of it here, is first the apparent *event* of coming to know our true nature, and then the apparent *process* of knowing it more clearly which follows. So far as I can tell, that unfolding is never-ending. I think it would have to be. Until we apparently wake up, our human insanity may be of one degree or another—caterwauling crazy, or modified and stratified—but it's never in question. If we are operating from an imaginary center as a make-believe, so-called separate being, there's simply *no way* to "get living right." There can't be, because we're wholly out of touch with reality. Life is just not about us! There's nothing personal about it!

If 7,000,000,000 people continue to operate from these make-believe individual centers, we will surely wipe ourselves out, along with many other species of plant and animal. This human insanity is either going to be addressed passively in the worst cataclysm the planet has ever seen, or it's going to be addressed actively as a population who's waking up, or both, but it is *not* going away, and it's now gone beyond the point where we can simply ignore it. The people in recovery are probably the best army we have to save our planet, simply because they represent relatively large numbers, and have a background in the price of insanity, and the reward of surrender; in honesty and openness. Either way things go, the ground of being won't be hurt one iota. It can't be. And one dream is as good as another. However, in a paradoxical twist, it has great meaning—*to us*. Enter another paradox. Nothing matters, but everything is important. Go figure.

Now let's get out of "theory," so to speak, and move into some mental experimentation. This inquiry and others can be extremely helpful in shaking us up, and waking us up.

Excercise 1: A Sense of Being

*

Go back to your childhood for a moment. Find a pleasant memory that happened between the ages of five and ten. Bring it clearly to mind. View the world just as you viewed it then, through the same eyes, so to speak. Put yourself in the scene. Is there not a sense of *aliveness*? You know you're *there*, in the scene. You can sense that you are *present*. You know that you are *alive*, that you *exist*. Clearly you had to have been present in that scene, because you recorded it. If you hadn't been there then, you couldn't play it back for yourself now. Experience the *sense of being* that you had as a child again right now. Just notice it.

Now find a pleasant scene that is halfway between that scene's time and this present moment. Get it clear in your mind's eye. Once again, view the world just as you saw it then, through the same eyes. Allow those feelings to come in, and feel yourself in that scene. Do you once again notice that you *know* you're there? There's a feeling, an awareness, a sense of *livingness*. You know you *are*. You know you're present. Experience the *sense of being* that you had in the middle of your life. Again, just notice it.

Now come to the present. Feel this moment, as you are reading these words. Stop and look around the room. You know that you *are*. You know that you exist. Even if you say, "I *don't* know it," there has to be someone or something saying that. You can't *not* know it. Something is experiencing this scene; something is reading the words here. That something is also seeing the room and everything in it. It may almost feel like something is *lighting up* the scene. One more time, just notice this present *sense of being*.

Now let's revisit both of the earlier scenes. Let's compare that pure sense of being, the pure *experience of aliveness*, of existence, that was there in your childhood scene with the sense of presence that you had in the second scene. Are they different? Look carefully if you must. I think you'll find the answer to be glaringly obvious, and I *don't* think you'll find them to be at all different. I believe you'll find the feeling of presence to be identical in both scenes. Now compare the sense of being from those scenes with the sense of existing, the sense of aliveness that you feel right now. Are the three different? I don't think so. I think you'll find that they are precisely the same.

Do you ever look in a mirror and wonder where the "younger you" went? That is the unchanging sense of being noticing the changing world. Change can only be noticed against a background of stillness. There can be stillness without change, but there cannot be change without stillness.

That pure sense of being remained *just so* all the way from childhood to the present. All the things in the scenes were different; everything *being seen* changed. But the thing that was *doing the seeing*, the underlying sense of being, *the thing that was doing the looking* remained the same. Stop and notice that. Don't work it over in your mind, don't start to intellectualize it, just notice that the sense of being remained constant amid vastly different scenes in completely different eras.

Now let's go back to that first scene, back to when you were a child. Is there not a feeling that the sense of existence was *always* there? Can you actually imagine there being a time when that sense of being did *not* exist? I don't think you can conjure up a sense of *not* being. The mind simply can't get there. Even if you imagine your birth, your birth didn't *invent* the world, did it? No, it was the mechanism by which that body-mind *joined* the ongoing world, but no more than that. Do you intuit that the sense of being was already present at your birth? We cannot imagine a time prior to our existence; it doesn't even compute. Our sense of being is not something that was ever born.

Come back now to the present, to sitting there reading this book. Notice once again that you are here, that you are alive and present. It's unmissable. Now, can you imagine a time when your sense of being, that aliveness you feel right now, will *not* be here? I don't think you can. Even if you imagine your death as being such a point, without an unchangeable something, the change we call death couldn't occur. Neither could the life that preceded it. We cannot imagine actually *not being*. Existence is not something that's ever going to die.

If you look at it closely, I think you'll agree that our sense of being at least *appears* to be eternal. There's no evidence that suggests otherwise, and there is at least *intuitive evidence*, brought about by our own investigation, that it is eternal. Eternity is not a lot of time, it is the lack of time. Eternity lies *outside* of time.

Let's introduce another line of questioning about this same sense of being. Where is the edge of it? Where are the *boundaries* to that sense of being? There *are* no boundaries to the sense of being; none at all. It is a boundless field. And where is its center? There is no center to infinity. Infinity is not a lot of distance; it is not a lot of space. Infinity lies *outside* of space.

Each of us knows we *are*. Each of can say "I Am" with identical authority, *using* our sense of being to speak *about* our sense of being. When a flower leans toward the sun, it is saying, "I Am." When a rock sits still in its rock*ness*, it is saying, "I Am." Every animal on the planet, from an insect to an elephant, by their very presence is also saying, "I Am." Stars do the same, and galaxies do the same. On a subtle level, every idea says, "I Am." Every thought, no matter how revolutionary or ludicrous, is also saying, "I Am." Because everything *is*. Regardless of their apparent differences, all things live in a homogenous commonality. All things are joined by it. Every wave in the ocean has more in common than it has in difference. Each of them are phenomena playing out upon noumena.

Perhaps we can best imagine these noumena as space. This space, the very space surrounding us right this very moment, is *alive*. It is brimming with energy. This all-accepting, ever-changing, all-binding, so-called empty space *is* "I Am." It does not exist *in* the now, it exists *as* the now. All things held within it are its mirrors; they are the face of no-face. We can call this pulsing, radiant I Am*ness*, this one thing going on, simply *what is* without the slightest bit of spiritual or religious undertone. What do spiritual or un-spiritual even *mean* in the all-encompassing, all-embracing Nonduality of not-twoness?

What is rules. To believe otherwise is to be insane. And we don't have to be crazy anymore; not if we don't want to be.

✳

CHAPTER THREE
Step Three

SURRENDER

ALL OF US WHO HAVE GONE THROUGH TWELVE STEP RECOVERY KNOW that the first three steps form the backbone of the entire recovery tradition. They are the vital foundation to a new life. We find the very same thing as we move into Nonduality. Surrender, however we see it, is the key. Let's touch on the first two steps one more time before we head into the all-vital third.

In the first step, as seen through the eyes we are using here, we began to "admit our powerlessness," by which I mean simply *noticing* that we are not in control of the universe, and never were. A story *within* reality doesn't actually have any control *over* reality. Here is where the lines leading *out* of Nonduality first form. No control? No thank you! We will see that things are not quite that cut and dried. Yet the bedtime story of control is just too sweet for many, even most, to give up, even for a moment. However, before you leave us and head for the manifest-your-own-amazing-rich-famous-life hills, let me say that while we cannot indirectly influence the *dream* of a "personal destiny" for our character, let me make one last plea for spiritual maturity. I'm not saying we are completely without choice. We're not. We have one *huge* choice, which changes our view on every other apparent choice. It is that choice which Nonduality is all about. We can change how we look at things—indeed, from *where* we look at things. Once again, when we change the way we look at things, the things we look at change.

In the second step we began to look into, and actually question, both our identity and our sanity. We can't question our identity *without* questioning our sanity, because our entire world view has been woven around the story of individual "me-ness." We are now beginning to actively open up to at least the *possibility* that we—and everybody we know—have been taken in by the power of collective conditioning, a sort of divine hypnosis. It hasn't been an all-bad ride, but now we'd like to at least *find out* what off-the-ride feels like. Until now, we never even entertained the *possibility* off-the-ride! After all, if we can't prove to our own satisfaction that there actually *is* a personal identity, and we have spent our whole lives *operating* from such a theoretical point, it's clear that *nothing* we have ever held dear or true could have been quite on the mark. If there's no center, and we've been pretending there is, then for goodness' sake, our entire view of world, self, the sacred and the profane, and *everything else*, has been completely askew. It *is* insane. Make no doubt about it: personal identity is the very dream we are being called to wake up from. This step is about coming out of the balcony seats and moving onto the spiritual stage.

The secret to the third step in recovery, at least as I lived and taught it for a long time, is turning over the conditions and outcomes of our lives to the Higher Power of our choice or invention—as they arise. That's what it's really about, and that turning over of our will, from a "me" to a better qualified "other", is a wonderful way to live, if we really live it. Many do in theory. Few do in practice. Still, even a partially committed movement in this direction is a damn big deal, and it's gotten many a person sober. Regardless of our level of commitment, that "turning it over" is the model, and there's no better, higher, or more beautiful way to travel through the dream state than that one.

In Nonduality we look at surrender from the other direction. Here we examine our most-sure, most-core addiction, which is our addiction to the dream of being a separate self. If we examine it closely, openly and regularly with honesty and humility, truth will begin to reveal itself, and that addiction will begin to thin and fade. The caveat here is that with rare exception we have to really want it in order for the fading to occur. As I've seen it, willingness is the golden key to ridding ourselves of all addiction.

This illusion of a separate self is the very dream that led us through the addict's hell for all those years. Once we fully see through the false idea of separation, of me-you-world-higher power—the notion of free will or destiny—*or surrender*—for an imaginary "me" completely drops away. Although philosophers and theologians have argued about free will versus destiny for centuries, indeed, for *millennia*, suddenly we, the common people in the ordinary world, are in a position to see for our very own selves that the entire conversation was, as Shakespeare said, "Much ado about nothing." The two sides kept each other from even asking the only pertinent question, which was, "Is there really an individual here to have, or *not* have a will?"

Of course we cannot just get behind a bit of persuasive book learning and say, "Okay, now I see. I don't exist as an independent, volitional being. Fine. *I'm* now going to run my life differently." This is the first reaction of many who resonate with these teachings upon first hearing them. There's nothing wrong with it, but if we closely examine the movement, just who is it that is now going to run your life differently? Surely it couldn't be the you that we're called upon to see through—could it? Slipping in on cat feet, ego has worked itself into the lead position of the charge to… see through ego. Ain't gonna happen.

First off, Nonduality is not about information; not in the end. We get enough information to *make a start for ourselves*, and then begin to rely on our own inquiry as much or more than we do outside teachings and teachers. We may continue to read and follow those who have gone before us, but this is a do-it-for-yourself program, regardless of all the paradoxes that introduces. Isn't it wonderful how paradoxes keep kicking sureness of its pedestal?

Nobody can give you this. Many can help, but the last mile is your own. So, rather than adopting a new belief, we simply try to suspend our belief in *all* such hearsay, i.e., "I exist" versus "I don't exist," pro or con. The dream has a million tentacles, and every one of them holds a spoon full of sleeping elixir.

Notice that any position about anything, pro or con, exists *only in the light of the other*. It's hot in here! How do we know? Because it's the opposite of cold! He's short! How do we know? Because his stature is the opposite of the guy we call tall! This is always the way of duality, and it's an easy way to spot if something is really true or not. If it's got an opposite, it's not really true. That includes every-thing in this book, too. I'm not telling the truth. I'm presenting, at the very clearest level that I can muster, something that points *at* truth. It could be said that I am lying at my very best!

If we already have a teacher, or we're already pursuing this teaching through books and other media, then we join our inquiry to those sources, but neither replaces the other. Each authentic intake method helps wipe fog from the others, even as it creates its own. As we begin to pull away the layers of ignorance on our own, then in all likelihood we will continually go back to living teachers and media to refine our personally gathered information and insights. This "lab work to field work, and back again" pretty well describes the method that's taught here. It's not the only way to truth, but it does have a good track record of success.

To the exact degree that our awareness of truth rises, so does our belief in ignorance— most notably a separate self—subside. There are infinite degrees in either direction, into either unconscious liv-ing, or conscious knowing. Hitler lived in the same era as Mahatma Gandhi. One lived in the dream, and the other lived in truth. One caused mountains of suffering, and the other brought mountains of relief. Suffering, relief. It's important for us to notice that Gandhi, who certainly knew his own true nature, still tended to those in the dream with the utmost care. Likewise Mother Teresa. Everything matters. Details count.

Just to be clear that we are not shutting any needed doors, let me step in and say that there's absolutely nothing wrong with a

completely dualistic cry to the heavens for help. I am in no way
suggesting that we discard prayer. We do what we do until we
do something else. I'm not even suggesting that sincere, heartfelt
prayer won't work for you. It *will*, in one way or another, even if
it only affects *you*. After all, prayer is a form of surrender. Within
the dream, which is where such prayer inevitably takes place, and
where any effects will occur, absolutely anything is possible. I
mean, once it's seen that *it's all spirit*, "impossible" ceases to be a
functional word in our vocabulary.

As we begin to move further in the direction of Nonduality,
we'll probably notice a shift occurring that moves us more toward
acceptance of *what is* and our adjustment to it, while relying less
on self-directed, petitionary prayer. At that point, our prayer has
become, "Help me to see the truth. Help me quickly and gracefully
accept what is already going on." However, we don't give up one
tool until we have another fully in hand. That would be taking a
purely intellectual view of Nondual teachings, which is like saying
that, after having thoroughly gone over the menu at a restaurant,
we're quite satisfied, and no longer need to eat.

It may not be as wise to compulsively design our spiritual program as it is to keep ourselves open, and then watch as it unfolds by
itself. If our earnestness is great, then as truth begins to sense itself,
and thus its apparently newly available options, much will occur on
its own. One of the odd things about Nonduality is that we find that
where we take our stand dictates how the world works. So long as
we are completely sold on duality, so long as that's how we see and
accept the world, then that's how life will show up for us. It's all
cause and effect stretching along a horizontal time line. When we're
doing inquiry, and thus questioning our own beliefs, we will notice
some loss of our old view's consistency. When our stories begin
to be shed, the field of possibilities begins to open. This is reality
getting its foot in the door. When we take our stand *as* awareness,
there is an immediate, total shift. It's no longer, "What you see is
what you get." It morphs into, "What you get is what you see." The
story will still unroll through apparent cause and effect, but we

might notice that some of these links are rather far-fetched! Reality seems to stretch.

Awakening often comes in waves. Something arises that is accepted as a problem, whereupon the world will show up as being completely dualistic—and negative. Personal involvement and suffering kick in, and we get to deal with that until we see through our ignorance into the truth of our being. Every time we see through our conditioning it gets a tiny bit easier to see through it in the next moment. At another time we may see straight from the heart of Nonduality, and find little or no anger, ugliness, or suffering. This is beautiful, and mightily encouraging, but let's not get attached to it either. Trying to hold it is precisely what will keep it at bay. When the shift has really deepened and matured, our experience of Nonduality is as consistent as was our experience in duality. There may be blips of unconsciousness, but these arisings are usually seen through almost as quickly as they arise.

That doesn't mean we're in a state of constant ecstasy; far from it. Enlightenment is not about an ongoing orgasm, or a hallucinogenic high. Awakeness is quiet bliss itself; it doesn't have to be constantly reinforced in the dream. I *love* the intensity of an immediate spiritual experience—after all, I still have an addict's hardwiring. Yet I've noticed that while there is the experience of quiet bliss when I'm sitting in my living room, incredibly, there can also be an embracing of *all* conditions. Well, sometimes yes, and sometimes no!

Here is a perfect example of third step surrender within trying conditions. A man was walking in a field when a tiger came up behind him, roared, and attacked. The man ran, but fell off a cliff. As he was going over the side, he grabbed a vine, which stopped his fall a few feet below the edge. The man looked up and saw the tiger circling above him. He looked down and saw two more tigers circling below him. Next he saw two field mice, one white and one black (perhaps named Yin and Yang?), beginning to chew away on his precious vine. It was a desperate situation. Just then he saw a single red strawberry growing from the cliff face. It gleamed in the sun, all red and green and gorgeous. He reached out, picked it, and popped it into his mouth. *Perfect*! So sweet! It was the best strawberry ever!

Our friend surrendered, without reservation, which doesn't mean so much that he brought his thinking into line with his situation, as it does that thinking spontaneously ceased on its own, allowing him to take advantage of the opportunities available *in that moment*. But he didn't surrender to three tigers, two mice, a thinning vine, and a looming, certain death. That combining of raw facts and projecting them into an imagined, "sure" future is just a story. That is the dream in action. Such a story might turn out to be accurate, or inaccurate, we never know. We *do* know that it's not true in the moment it is formulated.

The future is not fixed, and none of us can guess it. The *I Ching*, or the best psychic in town, may be able to see patterns coming together into a potential outcome, but no one can see into the future, because there's nothing to see into. "The future" is just an idea in our heads, and nothing more. It's *what isn't*. What we always "see into" is the now, as it arrives, literally as it reshapes and unfolds itself, on a moment to moment basis. If we pay just the slightest bit of attention we can see for ourselves that at the moment we begin to tell our story of future, we begin to suffer. Even if it's a *wonderful* future story—do you notice that it's *not here yet*, and how lousy this real moment we're living is in comparison to that make-believe moment we're not even living, and may never live, at least other than in our heads? Can you see that even in its birth we know the pleasant story will end, and there is latent suffering in that as well?

We have a new dog, a Shih Tzu we acquired through a rescue service, who got him out of a high-kill dog pound. He's the most adorable thing I've ever seen in my life. He's full of energy, incredibly funny, and adoringly affectionate. Ten minutes after falling in love with him I noticed my mind saying, "You won't always have him. He'll die and this specialness will be gone." My mind was offering me the opportunity to go ahead and suffer at the height of my joy. That's how it works. I'm grateful I don't have to take the bait any longer.

All of life is a constant interplay between freedom and restriction. The ancient Chinese knew this. The symbol for "crisis" in Chinese is composed of two figures, one representing "danger" and the other meaning "opportunity." We'll most often find the one for which we're looking. We all know that our apparent experience of life cannot last very long. Our stay here is a relatively short one. We can spend it in *doing*—worrying and warring, which are two methods of resistance, or we can spend it in *being*—peace and beauty, which are two aspects of surrender.

As we learn to trust and rest in peace and beauty, we can begin to let doing take care of itself. It will do just that. Isn't it interesting that although the majority of the world would tell you that they want peace and beauty, what would they have to confess to actually experiencing? Internal fear and war. There may be grand interludes between those two base levels, but the truth is, humans love fear, and they love war, and they will always return to them, at least until they don't. The proof is in the pudding. "Ye shall know the tree by its fruits," Jesus said. Let's look at why we, too, may secretly love fear and war, while finding peace and beauty to be threatening. What's our fruit and why?

When we are worrying or warring, there is a very strong sense of center. For real worry to take place there has to be a sure-thing-I who's doing the worrying about what might be going to happen to the sure-thing-I that we think we are. We're afraid of four things: we're not going to get something we want, we're going to lose something we do want, we're going to get hurt, or we're going to die. We might be mildly concerned about the welfare of some distant islanders confronted with a volcano or a tsunami, but we are *worried to death* over our own job, our lover's loyalty, and these damn shoes that don't quite live up to our expectations. We may still make a compassionate gesture appropriate to another's plight, but it's just not going to gnaw at us in the same way that our own difficulties do. No dilemma is quite so bad as *our* dilemma.

Certainly we are going to be concerned about our spouse being in the hospital, our child being out too late, or whether or not we're going to make the rent. Concern can lead to effective action, which is a good thing. But if we look closely, we'll see that actual *worry*, psychological suffering, arises only from a personal center, the imaginary "me," and that it in no way advances the situation. It's just wasted energy.

Our opinions are generally in conflict with reality. They are the means to suffering unnecessarily. Our opinion is layered *on top of* reality. It offers no benefit to anyone. This dropping is not something we can force. I am not advising you to "stop being judgmental" or even to "quit resisting life." What I am suggesting is that with the growing embrace of steps one and two, and continued inquiry, our center will automatically begin to loosen up. Loosening up is the first step in dissipation. Appropriate action will still happen, but without us being so stressed while it does. In fact, in the absence of interference, action will be both more efficient, and more effective.

Even when our opinion is in line with circumstances and events, if it's coming from a personal me, then that opinion and our peace are being held hostage to forces beyond our control. Any change of status could worsen our right-now-is-okay, conditional surrender. When we move beyond should and shouldn't and see that everything simply *is at it is*, that it's beyond need of our approval or dissent, then there is room for real, deepening peace. "Should" and "shouldn't" are fine words to use, but let's not believe them. *What is* exists beyond and below those sticky layers.

Just as worrying is automated resistance *by* the patterns inherent in an imaginary center, I define warring as defense *of* the center by the very same patterns. Ego found out long ago that the best defense is a good offense, so it goes to war as soon as it's wide awake, wars all day long, and stays at war almost to the point where the body drifts off to sleep. It may then war in the dream state, too. The specific acts of waking up and going to sleep are often the only two acts in our day that take place *out* of a state of war. This is because they cannot occur when resistance is present. Each of those events is the result of an unconditional letting go of one world for the other. In deep sleep there can be no war, because there is no "other."

We rehearse war—aggression and retribution—in our heads all the time, which means we're *acting out* war in our heads. Our bodies can't tell the difference between imagination and actuality, so they're constantly having to brace themselves by tensing muscles, flooding our systems with adrenaline and cortisol, revving up our hearts and lungs, perspiring and shaking. Amazingly, all of this can happen without anyone else even being in the room! It can be stirred up just from us rehearsing our fine "defense" of an imaginary future or past. We are constantly defending ourselves and our apparent possessions—our bodies, our self-images, our beliefs, opinions, and positions; our placement in the pecking order, our sexuality, our stuff, it's endless. We do it by striking *first*, which our mind erroneously and conveniently labels as being a response to threats known and unknown. We are *our own* biggest threat. We're daily killing ourselves and our planet, causing ourselves more strife and suffering than any imaginary army or assailant.

In every situation we always have the strawberry option. The strawberry option is simply to live *right now*, in that razor thin plane between what was and what might be. It is life devoid of story, free from past and future. It's a *simple* life. If we investigate, we can see that there is no more evidence for a past or future than there is for the separate entities. If it's seen, or even heavily suspected, that there's no separate entity, then we will also begin to see, or heavily suspect, that there is no past or future. Conversely, if reality begins to present itself from another side, and we begin to see that there is no past or future, then we will start to see, or deeply suspect, that there is no separate entity. No "me," no past or future. No past or future, no "me." No past, future, or "me," then there is just *this*—no problem.

Let's look at the claim for past and future. Let's start by noticing that we're investigating them *right now*, in the present. When else could we investigate them? There *is* no "when else." Ever.

There is always only now. Check it out for yourself. Think of a "past event." When are you seeing it? Now. Where are you seeing it? Here. Where else? Nowhere else, because there *is* nowhere else. This is just too simple for the mind to grab hold of. There is only now? There is only here? Those are the facts. If you try this same exercise with future, you'll get the same result. Past and future are mental constructs. The mind *cannot* grab hold of anything so simple with such huge ramifications; the mind can only *behold* it. When we are discussing past and future, we are once again dealing with polar opposites. Let's remember that polar opposites are the currency of the dream.

Tigers above us and tigers below *us* is a dream. It may be happening, but *who* is it happening to? Anyone? Is there a separate entity? In the absence of a personal me, is there a problem with tigers, a cliff, and a human being? In the absence of a personal me do we know what should happen? Do we know what is right or proper? Do we have a single shred of evidence that things should be any other way? And while we're looking at, what *is* actually happening in that scene? A strawberry is being enjoyed. That's *all*. It's just that simple. In the absence of a me, what's wrong with two mice eating a vine? They do it all the time! That's just *mouseness* at work, doing what it does. What's to worry about? Our fear stems not from the reality of an energy pattern named mouseness, but from the dream of a "me" in the center of the scene, a me that these white and black, yin yang little beasts are threatening. Beyond some paltry primal response by the organism, there is fearlessness. There's no *we* who are fearless; there is just fearlessness. There is just life, which cannot be injured or killed, added to, or subtracted from. There is just one thing going on.

This life is right in front of us. It's behind us, too! It's not up in our heads, it's down in our hands, it's surrounding our hands, it *is* our hands! In the world where our body is living, everything just is what it is, whether it's apparently pleasant or unpleasant, whether it's strawberries or sudden chest pains. This doesn't mean we fail to react. Like the miceness we spoke of above, *squirrelness* regularly attacks my bird feeder and I regularly respond to it. But there's no sense things should be otherwise, and thus there's no suffering in it. I throw food on the ground for them. I *like* squirrelness very much; I'm completely charmed. But I don't want it eating out of my feeder, because that's where the birds come. I neither resent squirrelness, nor ignore it. It's all fine, just as it is. And when it changes, that's fine, too.

Only when we begin to judge what *should* be appearing in our body's world, or our mind's world, do we begin to suffer, and we always suffer *personally*. Suffering cannot exist without something personal to attach to. Pain can and does, but not the psychological suffering that generally accompanies it. We can even suffer when we're knee deep in strawberries if we project that they won't last forever, or ask why we didn't have them yesterday, when we really, really wanted them, and should have had them. Psychological suffering is not a life strategy, it's just a painful story that we can live without—if we want to.

Let's push this just a tiny bit more. This really is the heart of it all. We can "get it" *right here, right now*. In fact, we'll never get it at any other time or place.

Understand. There is only *what is*. This is *it*. *This* present moment, *this* nonconceptual razor's edge, *this* current livingness is all that exists. Ever. There is one thing going on and it is constantly reshaping, literally constantly reforming itself—*as* itself and *for* itself. This very *what is* is all we ever have to surrender to, because it is the only thing we ever *can* surrender to! We cannot surrender to a concept! We cannot surrender to our own imagination. However, this now, this present experiencing, this *verbness* that is life, can *always* be surrendered to. If we examine it closely enough for long enough we may come to find that we have *already* surrendered to it! We might even find that we are surrender itself, and that this moment is apparently happening within the "open yes", the unconditional welcoming that we actually are. You'll have to look for yourself. I'm sharing here only what I have investigated and found to be true for me.

Let's have a drum roll, because I'm now going to tell some of my awakening story. Some people like that sort of thing, and some people hate it. I don't have an attachment either way. There was a time when I couldn't say *Hello!* to someone without sharing this, but that's been a long time ago. It rarely comes up now, whether I'm posting on my blog, or living my so-called life. I don't tell it here because it's a grand event that you should try to emulate. I didn't "do it," and neither can you. I did, however, do everything in my power to *encourage* it, and you can do that as well. Or not. There are schools of thought representing each side; you'll have to see which side you're drawn to. If you are drawn to the "nothing to do, and no one to do it" side of things, make sure that's a real draw, and not the lazy way out. Sometimes a personal leaning can *feel* like a divine pull, but it's *not* the same thing.

Regardless, this awakening story, like anybody's awakening story, is truly just a *story*. It's a story about a dream-man in a dream-situation who dreamed he woke up. Having said that, let me say that at the point in my life that it happened, it was the highlight of my dream! If I told you that it still was, it would be a sure giveaway that I wasn't currently awake. Why celebrate old memories when we can celebrate fresh life? All arguments aside, we may find some of my story instructive here, so I'll share some of it. I can provide no better first-hand example of a third step well taken, whether it's seen through either the eyes of recovery, or Nonduality.

A quick aside. We'll talk about the fourth and ninth steps when we get to them, but I will say here that my own first ninth step was, at least from a practical standpoint, completely botched. Details are not relevant, so let's just say that I did quite a "fearless and thorough" fourth step, as we are instructed, followed by an unhesitant five through nine. My sponsor at the time, who has devoted his entire life to this program, and who has sponsored a *nation* of men, told me I was the only guy he ever had who pushed him through working the steps, all of them, as quickly as we could.

I had done wrong. I knew it, and when it came to my ninth step I said so, while extending my earnest apologies. Those were my instructions from recovery literature, and that's what I did. Nowhere in our literature does it say that our amends process will end in our forgiveness. Mine didn't. I was arrested instead. I could fuss and tell you that shouldn't have been like that back then, but if I did, I'd have to suffer now, so I won't bother. In fact, it's probably the best thing that ever happened to me, even though even now I choke to write that down. But it's true. Given that I was determined to storm the Gateless Gate completely under my own steam, then without the kind of pressure a really ugly legal case put on me, I probably never would have woken up.

Back to our story. A couple of years after my arrest, with court now behind me, I was living in the bloody aftermath of my ninth step. Some would call it a "continuing amends." Okay. I just called it hell. For six months my weekends were spent in jail. I went in on Saturday mornings and got out on Monday mornings. My bookseller's income, always meager, was now slaughtered because I was unavailable to travel on the weekends, and couldn't acquire enough books to pay the bills. I also had to pay court fees, as well as the probation department for their supervision.

I was working terrifically long hours the other five days just to keep utter chaos, which was fully in command, from completely dismantling my tenuous life. I had an electronic monitor on my ankle so that my in and out times could be tracked. I was under heavy restriction. My little home, always my oasis, now had the atmosphere regularly shattered by probation agents. They were unfailingly polite, but nonetheless often came to my door, as they would come to any other door on their list: wearing pistols and body armor that had POLICE plastered all over it. It was all a wee bit shocking, let me tell you.

Above and beyond anything else, the situation was utterly *unbelievable*. To me, at least, and certainly to my wife, it defied any possible logic. Decades after the fact I was being treated exactly as if I'd committed a crime *yesterday*. The oh-so-active recovery guy was suddenly in a worse conventional fix than anyone he'd ever worked with. The little mystic in his book-lined living room would spend a morning or two a month talking to men with guns. It was nuts. Even one of my probation officers told me, "You know, Mr. Davis, you *really* should write a book about this." Here it is, Eugene.

Shortly after I was arrested, I came down with chronic, acute sciatica. The stress had to go somewhere, and it found my right leg, from hip to ankle. The pain was sharp and unrelenting. Toward the end of the acute stage, which lasted for several years, I couldn't stand for more than five or ten minutes at a time without moving into agony. Of course I made my living standing up: attending book sales in the field and packing books at home, so that was a serious complication. The pain was at its worst on the weekends, when I was allowed no pain meds, and was out walking the roadsides for miles, picking up trash with a county road gang,

In short, things got so bad that I lost all interest in life; it was simply more trouble than it was worth. I wanted *out*. My girlfriend's business partner (she is now my wife) had killed himself in 2002, and I'd helped her clean up the detritus from all of that, so I knew the kind of vast and crushing disaster that suicide leaves for the ones left behind. Killing myself simply wasn't an option for me. I wouldn't do that without her blessing, and she understandably wouldn't grant me her leave to do it—at least *not yet*. But it was certainly discussed, and the option was held open. If life didn't get better, then I could receive the blessing and shoot myself. I had a weapon already lined up.

So even though both body and mind were screaming fight or flight, I found myself in a position where I couldn't do either. In short, I was caught living a nightmare with absolutely no way out. I had *already* been surrendered to circumstances beyond my control; I just didn't see it that way yet. The facts were in, but the recognition was not. But it was right around the corner.

One morning, a couple of months into this ugly and grinding new lifestyle, I was sitting in my living room starting my day with spiritual readings and meditation. It was just like thousands of other mornings that I had spent the very same way. There was nothing special about that day. I had certainly been dramatically changed by all of those years of study and practice, and by having worked the steps to the best of my ability. Certainly no one could doubt my *earnestness*. I would scarcely have been recognizable even to people who knew me as recently as Portland. With all of that progress on the relative plane, insofar as the truth we are talking about here goes, I was as unconscious as I'd *ever* been.

On that day I was sitting in my big, stuffed chair reading a spiritual book. The author made a statement, followed by a question. It was something like, "Everything comes and goes. When everything else is gone, *what's left*?" I'd certainly run across that line of questioning before. But on this morning I read it and suddenly both my body and mind seized up, like I was a halibut that had been flash frozen. I felt something the size and shape of a BB turn 180 degrees in the very top, center of my head. That was *it*. Suddenly the curtain pulled back and my true nature—our true nature—showed itself with staggering clarity. The veil hit the floor. I could hardly breathe. It was absolutely *nothing* like I had expected.

Suddenly everything, absolutely everything came clear to me in a rush. I suddenly knew the answer to a hundred spiritual questions, all in a single moment. Oneness was dancing! *I* was dancing! *I* was oneness! My God, *what is* was seen to be so bright and *big*!

While the seeing in Portland had carried a seed of the same truth that this awakening did, what I'd thought was the whole enchilada was now recognized as having been minor, just a tiny taste by this new standard. It had been but a glimpse! *This* unveiling, so much larger and clearer, felt "completely complete." But so had the glimpse in Portland! Now I know that they always do, every one of them, large or small.

My 2006 awakening was *not* complete, but it *was* large, so to speak, and it *did* cut deep. The aperture of awareness remained quite wide open for several days, and half-open for weeks, or months. It has never completely closed again. Actually it had never *completely* closed since the Portland event. But where there had been a dot of light there was now a major crack that has since widened. We just can't *unsee* what we see. For the curious, a second awakening occurred about fifteen months later. In the first awakening we could say that I saw clearly what I *am not*. That's what I deem "the 180," because reality is exactly the opposite of what we've imagined, even for those of us who've read hundreds of books. No one is ever prepared for it. They can't be, no matter how well read or practiced they are. I saw that I was not a separate entity, that there was no such thing as a separate entity. There was one thing going on. Period.

It's really hard to remember all the details, but if what I'm about to say isn't true, then it's as close to the truth as I can get through memory. In that awakening I knew I was the one thing going on. I could see that very clearly. But other than for a brief period, I didn't *feel* what I knew. I knew what I wasn't. I knew what I was. The difference between knowing and feeling is large, though it may not seem so as you read this. It's profound.

In the second awakening we might say that I saw clearly what I *am*. I now deem this second movement the 360, because we've come all the way back around. While I *knew* in the first apparent event that was the one thing, it didn't register in my gut. In that second seeing, I was everywhere. Everywhere I looked, I saw me. Everything was the face of God, from water to walls to watches. I don't mean just visually. There is a powerful knowing that pulses through the body, a body now grown as large and boundless as the universe. All of this defies description, and I can't say anymore about it that will make any sense at all.

All of this is reported via hindsight, and there really is no accurate hindsight reportage of these kinds of spiritual experiences. You're in it, or you're not. What I do remember is the slow fading back in of a "me" to whom all of this was happening. There was now a "me" *seeing* a "that," where before there had been a complete absence of "me-ness," and only life *being* itself, with itself, for itself. This is my poor description of what is known as the "witness state." It's not nearly so subtle a difference as it may sound. Duality is duality, subtle or profound. Now, years removed, I can't honestly tell you what, over the next weeks or months, was ongoing and what was memory. I just don't know. My ordinary life remained completely chaotic, and now this was added into the mix. This was the great comforter, of course, but it was still confusing.

I used that awakening the way a carpenter uses a hammer. When I was in jail, I would sit on the floor in a half-lotus position with my eyes closed in the hallways as we waited to be let in, let out, or searched. I was using it to escape. It's understandable and forgivable. I began to see myself as this special guy, whose life was beginning to sound a lot like Job's. Even in the sway of oscillating awakeness, ego was rebuilding under the disparate guises of "victim" and "special." It took a very long time for that to fall away. Given the choice, would you rather be a misjudged mystic, or a common criminal? Do the math. As I reflect on it now, it all runs together, like scenes from different movies arbitrarily sewn together. If I wasn't making a central point with all of this, I probably wouldn't bother to relate it. Reading about someone else's awakening is about as useful as hearing about someone else's orgasm. We can sense it was exciting for *them*, but once again, what about *us*?

The take-home point here is the intense, even overwhelming sense of restriction that was followed by an explosion of freedom. Consider this: two walls are moving toward you. You can see that you're just about to be crushed to death. Yet you can't go forward and you can't go back. What do you do? *Nothing*. And that's precisely the point. Surrender *happens*.

The people who run monasteries, at least the people who've run them who have been so-called awakened beings, have known about the results of these polar opposites, and have employed this strategy for millennia. They used dream mechanisms to move people beyond the dream. However, when it's constructed instead of growing organically out of situation, it isn't as efficient. A whole lot more people go into monasteries seeking enlightenment than find it. For many others, a monastery is simply a damn fine place to hide from life. There's nothing particularly spiritual about it, but it's a *really* effective hideout. There's nothing ego likes better than a costume and a spiritual storyline. Funny hats are a plus.

In my opinion, the primary role of spiritual practices is simply to wear the seeker out. As I see it, there's little chance that we're going to directly practice our way into enlightenment. Inquiry would almost be an exception to that, because it's a direct investigation into the nature of reality, and illusion can't stand up to it over the long haul. Just as with the example above, with inquiry we use the mind to get beyond the mind; we employ the mechanism of the dream to move beyond it. The mind will take us to the landing just outside the Gateless Gate. We then have to be invited inside. So even inquiry has its limits.

What frequently happens with practices is that the seeker becomes caught up in the means, while conveniently forgetting about the end. We become deep readers, wonderful meditators, and we can stand on our heads, all of which are just fine, they simply have little to do with reaching enlightenment. It's also a great way to take on a new identity, the new me with my special costume, or gear, and my highminded spiritual storyline that will completely *prevent* enlightenment. It's the new, smart, sincere, "spiritual" me versus the old, foolish, "unspiritual me." I should know; I'm an expert. I've done this about forty times. I could do it again tomorrow; you never know. There's no place to stop and call the game over. This is the ride that never ends, and the flower that is always opening, but never fully blooms.

Once it's really seen that no amount of meditation, chanting, specialized breathing, drumming, prostrating, posturing, praying, reading, kneeling, dancing, or whatever the hell else has been dreamed up for seekers to do, is going to break down the Gateless Gate, then we are stuck seeing that we simply *can't do it*. I say this as someone who has read, sat, chanted, prayed, kneeled, and postured. Somehow I missed out on drumming and dancing, but I didn't miss much else, and who knows? I could take them up tomorrow, and it's fine if I do.

In my case it took every bit of what it took; it takes what it takes until it takes, as they say in the rooms. But I started out *assuming* it was going to take all of that, and I started out *assuming* it was going to take a long time. If we start believing it's going to take a lot of practices over a long period of time, guess what? It will. We always get what we really want. What we really want may not be what we *think* we want, or what we *say* we want, but in the end, what we really want will show up. With or without a glimpse, enlightenment may never happen at all, or at least in this life. There are a lot of people wandering around who run hot for a long time, but who finally just give in to inertia and a lovely spiritual lifestyle while relinquishing the core objective. I get it. I did *that*, too!

I'm simply suggesting that we might not want to *begin* by deciding in advance what it's going to take to "become enlightened," or to "be enlightened." If we are honest, we can see that we probably *don't know*. This "I don't know" can be a hard thing for egos to take, but it can also be very useful. Taking a mental position locks us into a viewpoint. A viewpoint can only stem from a center. Starting out *at* the center to try and *overcome* the center may not be the most skillful method. Within "I don't know," we will float more freely. It will save us a lot of time.

Let me share something with you, something you may find remarkable. I live in South Carolina, which is the belt buckle of the Bible Belt of America. There simply is not much interest in Nonduality here. Oh, I occasionally hear from holdouts around the state; I'm not saying there is *no* interest here, only that there is not very much. I've never had more than a couple of in-person students at a time, and I grew every single one of those myself. I didn't do it on purpose; I wasn't out to hatch any new Nondualists, but it can't help but happen. It's just the nature of the teachings.

My point is that I've seen two friends of mine, on separate occasions, neither one of whom even knew there was *such a word* as "Nonduality," come to an awakening while we were talking, just doing some elementary inquiry, without their even knowing what it was we were doing. I don't mean I tricked them, they knew I was up to *something*, and they trusted me, so they willingly went along. But from their blessedly innocent view, they were just talking to their buddy Fred, and he was simply asking some questions in his weird, spiritual way. It was no big deal. Until it was! Granted, it was just a good glimpse for each of them, but never underrate the piercing nature of a short shot of grace. My friends didn't have any Nondual concepts for me to *overcome*. I think this was the critical factor, this and their trust in me. My point is that it didn't take a lot of esoteric practice, or the acquisition of any special knowledge. It didn't take a long time. One of them had been "studying" Nonduality for about an hour with me before he woke up. The other had been fed some Nondual principles over time, but they were classified as such.

The recovery of your absolute identity is a staggering and often life-changing experience, whether you initially recover it for a second or a lifetime. One of my friends maintains an active interest in this teaching, though he had no interest or experience with Nonduality prior to that day. The other has more or less dropped from my view, but he called the other day, and he still, at least, remembers. That "memory," however, can get us in trouble, because we take things seen from the absolute view and try to apply them to the relative world. It doesn't work. Whether they stick with this thing, or find they can walk away from it, I *can* tell you that it's set something in motion that won't end until both of those bundles have completely seen through illusion and embraced reality. Everybody wakes up in the end. It only avoidable for just so long.

On a *secondary* level, however, let me go on record as being *very much in favor* of practices. Prior to enlightenment, practices prepare body and mind for conscious hosting of truth. Fertile ground makes all the difference in how well a thing grows. Meditation brings a calmness that's quite useful for inquiry. We can't do a whole lot of meticulous inquiry while we're being constantly distracted by obnoxious demands. It's also great as surrender, allowing awakeness to do its work with us without much interference. What's often called True Meditation, which we'll talk about later, is great for its own sake. Every practice has its benefit. These weren't invented by fools, and they aren't used by fools today. Many of them are highly skillful, especially as passed on by awakened teachers.

And of course, "practices" include reading! Prior to enlightenment books give us a building context. The people who think context isn't important are the people who don't have any. Books help the mind get used to these alien ideas that put the experience of our everyday life under suspicion. In post-enlightenment books become traffic cops, helping us find an orderly path in confusion. They also help to increase insight and context, particularly for those who feel called to share. Not everyone does. Some people are teachers, some people are not. Teaching is more about the ability to communicate effectively than it is some supposed higher level of enlightenment.

So, if some of us already do some of these practices, great, let's keep it up so long as we are drawn to them. But please don't think that if you do so-and-so *then* you'll surely wake up. The "then" alone is enough to hold you back forever. Enlightenment happens now, right now, only now, over and over, again and again, within the *eternal* now. It's not a cause and effect thing, and it doesn't happen within the apparent stream of time. We are enlightened to *this* moment, to *this* arising, or we are not enlightened at all. That opening we once had, that connection and bliss we felt for an hour, or a day, or a week, was really great, but there's one thing we can easily notice about it. *It's gone.*

Spiritual experiences come and go. They're terrific! I have quite a few more I could tell you about. And then you could tell me yours. But we wouldn't have done anything but entertain ourselves with yarns of yesterday. In the end, every spiritual experience is "the one that got away." They are as real as anything else, but all arisings pass. They come from, exist in, and then return to awakeness, the one thing going on. Spiritual experiences are fleeting; awakeness is not. What we're discussing here, in this teaching, is the one thing that *doesn't* come and go. It's the one thing that doesn't move. It doesn't wax, or wane, age, or die. It is the one thing going on that watches all things come and go, that watches them move, that watches them wax, wane, age, and die, and which simultaneously *is* all those things, all at once, at every stage of their beingness.

This brings up something quite tricky that we need to address head on. Most of us have come here from recovery. We are addicts by nature. We are seekers by nature, which is what addicts are doing. This spiritual seeking is the biggest game of all. The consequences of spiritual addiction are unlikely to wreck our lives, or put us in a hospital or jail. In a way, it's worse. I say that because we will have actually brushed up against truth, seen it, tasted it, and then turned our heads in one more drive for self-centered pleasure and escape. I don't need to spell all of this out for us; we *know*. We know what addiction is, we know that we're prone to it, and that there is always a steep price for indulging it. What I'm saying is that we need to know to watch out for this particular *brand* of it.

Spiritual experiences can easily become quite a keen addiction. We can seek them out for the bliss and the mental glory, from retreat to retreat, around the country and around the world. It really shines up our story to think of ourselves as being so spiritual and so special. "Whew! I meditated until my knees blew out! How about *that*!? Am I cool, or *what*? No, I didn't wake up, but I'm sure I will pretty soon. I was really close, I know that much."

The body remembers the physical bliss and rushes of energy. This has always been the focus of the addictive personality. The mind remembers the great high, where everything is funny and everything is new. It's the best, most powerful drug of all. And another drug addiction is just what our spirituality can become.

After a line of intensives and retreats, we are still looking for the next teacher who will be able to give us a hit of shakti energy, or another glimpse of truth. We are so sold on the drug that we propel right past actual awakening. Over and over we throw away the meal for the sake of an appetizer, until finally, hopefully, we notice that we're not going anywhere, unless, perhaps, it's backward. There's no standing still in spirituality. You're always in motion, headed one way or the other.

The cure for this brand of craving is to put the seeking down, and *start living what we have already learned*. It's a short-circuit for ego, and it prepares us for receiving more. The spiritual path is much like the secret agent path: it's all on a need to know basis. We get what information we need when we need it, and not before. We do not, as a rule, learn the highest or most subtle truths first; we work our way through layers of ignorance, and then conditional truths in order to reach them. Insights build on insights. This does not happen simply by racking up more and more knowledge, but by allowing truth to penetrate, and by putting our insights to work in our lives.

We can resist enlightenment a long, long time. That's an addict's nature. I was so resistant about my chain-smoking that I used to tell people, "This goddam *breathing* is interfering with my *smoking*." I loved being the poster child for resistance. Not anymore; it's too painful. I quit smoking ten years ago, by the way.

The path of non-resistance, esoteric as it may seem, is really quite practical. As we begin to act in accordance with what we know, when we move toward allowing oneness to guide our relationships, our work, and our conduct, we'll find ourselves more frequently receiving sharper, clearer insights along the way. And we'll notice that something new is completely taking us over. This may sound scary, but in my case it's been beautiful. Life is so much smoother, so much calmer, so much more enjoyable. We can see love working in our lives and taking care of us in a million little ways. We feel it. We *know* it. We've entered early retirement!

This step, as seen through the eyes of recovery, is all about consciously relinquishing our will and reconciling ourselves with the one will there actually is. However, in actual practice, we often fall into employing surrender only after our worrying and warring have already failed us. That's fine for a while. We do what we can do when we can do it, and all of us have failed in order to qualify for membership in our fellowships. But as that egregious failure of personal power begins to fade in memory, and our lives begin to perk up and straighten out, the third step frequently becomes our back-up plan. After all, what if our Higher Power doesn't know how things should really go for us? Might it not need our aid or advice?

In Nonduality, at least as it is presented here, this third step is not the *back-up* position; it is the *only* position. In Nonduality we see that the one will is simply another name for *what is*. There is just one thing going on. The deep concern for our own little personal agenda begins to drop to the side as being unnecessary and inefficient. Our available energy becomes more devoted to recreating us as a more transparent body-mind, through which the light of truth can more easily shine. It's not something we actually *do*; it's more like something we *allow*. On a cloudy day the sun is hidden until a fair wind blows the clouds away. When we allow it, paradoxical as this may be, Nonduality is a fair wind that blows like a gale.

What we're doing here is simply seeing that whether we're dealing with traffic, ball games, financial challenges, relationships or weather, it's our attachment to specific conditions and outcomes that causes our suffering. It's our arrogant, erroneous belief that we have knowledge of what's right and what should be. We are hung, or blessed, as we see it, with *what is* one hundred percent of the time. Everything is just as it should be *until it's not*. We continue to take action as situations dictate. We act in this moment to bring about what we feel is right in the next, but we don't do it from the ground of resistance. We do it from the ground of surrender, and then the snatching and consoling take place quickly, smoothly, and effectively.

I will tell you a quick story about how this action can take place. A friend of mine came to visit one day. He had a new little puppy, a toy poodle; the cutest thing you ever saw. We thought his dog should meet our old dog at that time, who was a sweet, lazy old golden retriever named Gus, who never had a bad thought in his life. So we put them together on the ground in front of us. Two seconds later Gus snatched that puppy up in his jaws and put his head rearward in a backswing. We'd had another golden before this one, who was quite the ratter. I knew this was how they killed small animals: they broke their necks with blinding speed and efficiency.

I never thought. I didn't even know I had moved. But suddenly I found myself on Gus' back, completely immobilizing him while my hands went to his jaws and pried them open. The little poodle was scared to death, but unharmed. Half a second longer and that dog would have been dead. With no Fred there to slow it down, the body instantly saved the day. For my friend and me, it took us time to actually register and catch up to the events, for they were over as quickly as they started. We looked at each other in wonderment at what we had just witnessed. Neither dog was hurt a lick.

Let me repeat: surrender does not mean a lack of action. It means *a lack of interference* with the one will's action. I have to say this over and over again, because it's a constant complaint of those who just cannot follow what is being said here. I am not saying that we give up our control and thus gain both peace and efficiency of effort. We never had control. The truth is, of course, that there *is* no separate entity to either have control, or not have control. Taking one side or the other leaves us as lunatics in an asylum arguing over which one key would let us out if only we had one. I fully understand this *misunderstanding*, but it is nonetheless nonsense.

I remember how happy I was when a woman at a recovery meeting gifted me a little gold stick-pin. I still have it. It reads, "Don't give up. Surrender." I was *so happy* that someone was hearing what I was saying!

We already have a working model of just how things should be at every given moment. We call it life; we call it *what is*. Without our projections, comparisons, and expectations, life is simply *present*. We're always looking at a done deal. By the time our sense organs conceptually present what we call "the present" to our minds, we are effectively viewing the past. How do you argue against a case that's already been won? There is only *what is*. And this *what is*, which *already* is, stands *as it is*, and there is no suffering in it, because it's not about us. *It's about itself.*

It's good to start noticing that we do not and cannot successfully direct our actions and conditions. We are not the boss of *what is*. Don't take my word for it. Honestly look at your own experience. Certainly there is the *feeling* of control; that's part of the play. But if we're in control, why didn't we quit our addictions when we first knew we should, and said we would? Because we had a disease?

Is this disease the single exception to our theoretical control, or is it in fact the star witness in the case against autonomy? I suggest it is the latter. But our addictions are just an example; the available examples are endless.

If we control our thinking, why would we ever think things that make us feel bad? If we control our actions, why would ever say or do anything to hurt a loved one? How come we're not happy every moment of every day? Are we choosing to think sad and mean thoughts? Are we really? We relish talking about the thing we planned or predicted which actually happened. Okay, sometimes we can spot how a pattern might apparently evolve and make an educated guess. But how about all the times our predictions and projections did *not* come through? We don't brag about those. We hardly notice them. We don't want *others* to notice them either! The emperor has no clothes! So we sweep our many misses under the rug. And we go right on lying to ourselves.

Sometimes I head for the kitchen for tea, and find myself in the living room straightening books instead. I think I changed my mind, that I directed this change in my course, but if I look back I can see that actually I didn't even think up the thought that I wanted tea to begin with! It just popped into my head, and then my brain *processed* it. I finish straightening the books and head for the kitchen again. The cat whines, so I lean down to pet him. When I do that, I notice my shoes are untied, so I tie them. And then I remember the email I was supposed to send and didn't, so I rush up to the computer. I never got my tea. Control? No. Conditioning meeting circumstance.

And here's the thing. Everything happened exactly right. I didn't forget my tea by mistake. It was all part of *the* plan, it just wasn't part of *my* plan. I say "plan" with a wink, because in truth it's all happening spontaneously, every bit of it. I don't need to understand it to work with it, or rather to happily allow *it* to work with *me*! There is a plan-less plan just like there is a Gateless Gate.

Earlier this evening it felt like I decided, "I really must write tonight." Did I really decide that? Where did that decision come from? Am I choosing my thoughts, or just hosting them? I want to think I am in charge, it feels to this body like it's in charge, but it's been quite clearly seen, that such is *not* the case. We are the lamps through which raw electricity is directed as it travels to a light bulb. But it's the *bulb* that's shining brightly, *not* me. I am cut on, and I am cut off, by a switch I cannot control. All the time in between those two events I do what I do, as a follower and not a leader. There is just *one* will, and even that is a manner of speaking. In this case, Fred's body is in the study, and there is certainly *typing going on*, but there's no one here—no separate entity, no story-ness actually doing it. Fingers are flying, and words are coming out with a certain tone to them. Fred*ness* is hard at work. But none of this is directed by a me; it's all spontaneously arising.

Our body-minds react to ever-changing events and conditions with an ever-changing set of mentally rehearsed plans, *none* of which may occur. However, that's no problem, because we'll claim whatever *does* arise as having been our own plan—*after the fact*. Our upbringing, DNA, and a billion other regional micro-processes are effectively "in charge" of us, and trillions of others are in charge of everything surrounding us. There's *no one* actively in charge. This ship is sailing along on its own while I madly declare I am the captain!

I love to think I am the master strategist who keeps my book company rolling. It's a particularly attractive story. But I certainly don't *believe* that story. Reality is all too clear. For years I've been rescued *in advance* and *despite* my various strategies. I've been openly reporting that to my wife for the last five years. Now she can see it herself. The biggest challenge in what I do for a living is acquisition. I have to be able to get great books, and I have to be able to buy them cheaply enough that I can sell them for a profit. Every single time one mode of acquisition dies out, I notice that another mode was born months *prior* to that final event, when my ongoing source dries up and blows away. The new method is inevitably already in place, easier and more stable, requiring less time and effort on my part, which frees me up build relationships with teachers, dialogue with seekers, edit my blog, and write this book, all in the *conscious* service of the whole. The body's circumstances are conforming to bring efficacy to its new tasks.

I know I've already touched on some of this, and I'll be touching on it again before we're done. The repetition you find here and in most Nondual teachings is not accidental. Virtually all of us have to have the utterly obvious pointed out over and over again before truth finally begins to dawn *to itself*, and of its own accord. Talk to the awakened, or read their stories. What do they say about their apparent awakening event? Again and again we hear some variation of, "When it happened, I suddenly saw that it had been there all along—right under my nose!" What we're looking for is already present, but we can't see the space for the forms. Repetition helps us pull away the layers of not only our own direct conditioning, but the conditioning that we came hardwired with, which we call DNA. It's the wonder-software that makes us what we are, but that doesn't mean it's not blind to reality.

Regardless of what tradition we're following, so long as we believe in separate, autonomous "me-ness," there is no way on earth we're going to be able to even remotely live up to this step's true calling. As we begin to relinquish our addiction to self, *what is* can be seen to be all that's left. When it is clearly seen in any situation that there is no alternative to the totality of what already is, surrender is automatic; we need take no action at all. And with that automatic surrender of the personal me, guess what? The personal me's attachments begin to fade. There's nothing solid for them to attach to! You don't drop your attachments, your attachments drop you! This is the real truth of genuine renunciation. Dispassion is not a goal for us to reach for in order that we may become more holy and come to a future awakening; they are a side effect of our opening to truth, and waking up right now, as unholy as convicts. It's something that comes with the territory.

Let's get back into personal exploration. I have two exercises for us, one of them is short, the other is not so short. But both are helpful in our proving to ourselves the living truth of Nonduality.

Excercise 2: Noticing What We Don't Notice

*

Close your eyes. Now hold up your hand to what you know is eye level. Now, open your eyes. What's the first thing you see? Unless you are the first exception I've ever run across, you answered, "My hand." It's the obvious answer, is it not? But it's not the first thing you saw. The first thing you saw was *space*, but you didn't notice it! We are blind to what actually *is*; seduced by our vision into choosing form over formlessness. We look right through space before finally settling our attention on an object, do we not? Take a peek. Even visually there is a whole lot more space around than there is form. But underneath the surface, there is more space. The great majority of every person, every object, even of the universe itself, is acknowledged to be formless space, yet form gets almost all our attention. The only reason a cup or a house is useful is because of the space they hold. If our hearts and lungs weren't empty, they'd be useless. Still, we push it to the side in favor of something objective. And we never even notice the subjectivity that is looking. It has a lot in common with that space.

*

Our true nature is more akin to space than form. We've spent our entire lives looking at a tiny fraction of the universe, because we are hypnotized by objects. We are hypnotized by mental objects, too, by which I mean thoughts. All the while the thoughts are occurring inside of overlooked, underrated spaciousness. Objects get all of our attention, but space always forms the stage. This is not *quite* true, but it's true enough, and for the moment we will say that space is the screen for the movie of self and world. More importantly, it is also the projector!

From where I sit, our true nature unquestioningly *is* much more like space than it is like form. Notice that our bodies are "contained" within space. Each of us thinks of ourselves as being the subject of all objects, but interestingly enough, to everyone else our body is an object within *their* subjectivity. Everyone is the center of the universe, but only to themselves.

In Buddhist mythology there is the story of Indra's Net. In ancient times Indra was said to be the king of the gods and the ruler of the heavens. He had a net of jewels, with a diamond at every juncture. Each diamond reflected all the other diamonds. Our planet's population could also be said to be something like a mobile Indra's Net. Everyone else is our object, and we are theirs. As a provisional truth, we could say that if each juncture, each person is a reflecting jewel, then the net itself is composed of space. Perhaps you've heard the story of the fish who went swimming around asking all the other fish, "Where's the water? How do I find the water?" Such foolishness, we think! But we're doing the same thing in our quest for enlightenment, or a better "connection" with God. The only thing stopping us from finding them is our *search* for them. Our real challenge in our spiritual search is one of simple recognition. I am not saying that our true nature *is* actually space, but I'm saying that if for now we *envision* it as such, then we can plainly see that any step that pretended to be taken in the direction of the divine, would actually be a step *away* from the divine, which is already here. We can't find more spaciousness than we already have. This big change up in our thinking can be the precursor to our recognition of what the awakened tell us is right under our nose.

We are right back to talking about addiction, are we not? We are addicted to objects and to searching. Like all addictions, there's a price to be paid. Maybe we should begin to take notice of space as well as objects. Mind wants us to choose a side and stick to it. The ground of being must be *either* form *or* formlessness, it argues. But that's only the mind's natural duality. What does even the most casual investigation prove? Form and formlessness are like the flip-sides of our reality, only we pay great attention to one side, and completely ignore the other. Here we are suggesting that we look at *both* in order to find something beyond either.

In this same way, let's start looking at what is already here. Not in some cosmic way, but in an actual, practical, put-your-hand-on-the-desk sort of way. Let's see if we can begin to move from the either-or model of thinking to the both-and model of seeing and being. This will become more clear as we move along the hypothetical path.

If there is one thing that consistently blinds us to our true nature, it's the body. We love our bodies *so* much! After all, we've always considered them to be "us." At the very least we've thought they *contain* us. We are separate entities, and we are our bodies, or we somehow "dwell" in the body. This idea is so firmly entrenched that it goes unquestioned. We are going to question it here. As nice as it would be, few will take this inquiry and suddenly see the truth. But just so you know, it *can* happen, and it *does* happen. It was through this inquiry that I saw my two friends "pop off," as teachers sometimes call it when folks get a good glimpse. Their *body* attachment returned within a few seconds (although their minds were on some level changed forever), but even that body attachment got thoroughly shaken, which is both illuminating and encouraging. We shouldn't downplay the power of encouragement; it can be a big deal for us, especially when it's first-hand.

We have always had exclusive identification with a specific body-mind. The first Nondual jump, which is a big and important one, and which typically follows a spiritual experience of varying levels, is usually a shift from this body identification to that of believing ourselves to be a witness-in-the-body. We no longer think of ourselves as a body, but rather as spirit, *held within a body*, witnessing a play or movie, which is taking place *outside of* the body. It's an important step, but we don't want to confuse a *step* with a *landing*. This is a phase. It can be difficult to overcome, especially if we're lazy.

I'm presenting this next inquiry as a story, and I'm going to use myself as the example, simply for the sake of efficiency. This way

I can share my own experience with you, and the experiences of others that I've shared this with during spiritual dialoguing, plus it just comes out on the page more smoothly. Please don't take this as a simple read-and-remember exercise. You really need to do this inquiry yourself so that you come up with your own answers. I'm not holding out on you. The "good stuff" doesn't come later. This is the good stuff. People have woken up from *this exercise alone*.

As I tell this story, stop after every question, and after every "loss," or cut, and direct the questioning toward yourself. Question and probe—where are you? My wife is a woodworker, and she says, "If you want to make furniture, you have to cut some wood." What she's telling us is to get out of our imaginations, out of spectatorship, and into involved action. It's very good advice.

Excercise 3: **Where's Fred?**

*

If someone asks me, "Where's Fred?" I'm going to point at my body. Where else would I point? It's the only logical place to point, is it not? But is it true? Inquiry is always dedicated to one thing: discovering truth.

What part of my body is *me*? The whole thing, right? So what happens if I lose my left hand in an accident? Am I still me, am I still *as much* me, as I was before? There's less of me here, so if the body is me, how can I still be as much me as I was prior to losing my hand? And what about the hand itself? I just said a moment ago that my hand was part of me. Suddenly I'm changing horses in midstream and saying, "No, they're just incinerating my cut-off left hand. I'm still over here, as much me as ever. Fred is now *what's left* of this body!" Notice how the mind is happy to reconstruct its story to go along with changing facts. The mind couldn't care less about facts. All it wants is a story. A story is enough to keep a center in place.

On the way home from the hospital, let's pretend I'm in another accident. This time I lose not only my right hand, but my whole right arm! Clearly, it's going to be a tough day for me. So where am I now? My dimensions have changed. My weight has changed. My description and capabilities have changed. Still, I am claiming again to be what's left of my body, even though what's left is significantly less than it was just a little while ago. And the same question comes up about incineration. What is it they're burning up? Is that "old me"? Is this still viable part the "new me"? If feels like I'm simply *still me*, the one over here with the slowly disappearing body. Both the hand and arm are now medical waste. Burn them up in a hurry before they begin to stink and hatch bacteria that make us ill! They used to be me, but they are now *not* me. Their me-ness had more to do with *location* than it did any inherent qualities.

Just as they're wheeling me out of the hospital, a truck comes along and smacks my wheel chair. They rush me back inside and amputate my legs. I tell them, "To hell with it, take that funky handless arm, too." And they do.

Well, heck, now I'm in quite a fix. I'm a head and a torso, and nothing more. Someone comes along and asks a nurse, "Where's Fred?" She points to my bed, of course. My visitor, a guy I've known for a long time, leans over and looks at me, but doesn't recognize who he sees. After all, the Fred he knew had four appendages. "Where's Fred?" he asks.

"It's me," I tell him. "Look at my face and you'll see it's me."

"You look a lot like Fred in face," he says, "but Fred had arms and legs; I distinctly remember them."

"Well," I tell him, "I *lost* my arms and legs in a couple of accidents. They're incinerating them to keep them as medical waste. They *were* me, but they're not me anymore, because they're no longer in the right location to qualify as being me."

"So Fred doesn't live in those arms and legs any longer?" he asks.

"Nope."

"Did he ever?"

"Oh sure," I say. " I used to live there as well as here, but now

I just live here. It's the same house, sort of. You could say I've been downsized."

My friend is something of a skeptic, and he's not so easily convinced. He's also rich with a penchant for gambling. "I'll give you a million dollars if you can prove to me that Fred is in what's left of that body," he offers. "If you can't prove it, I'll take everything Fred owned in exchange. Is it a deal?"

I take the bet and call my surgeon, who by now knows me pretty well! I offer to share the million bucks if he'll help me win this bet. "All you have to do is *cut*," I say. "We'll find the real me in here," I say, pointing downward with my chin. "Operate and we'll show him, Doc."

I guess my doctor is short on both money and scruples, so he agrees. It's my money and my body (maybe!). He is, in fact, a little curious himself. No one's every brought anything like this up before. It's intriguing. He gives me a big load of local anesthetic so that I can follow the action. He hands both my skeptical friend and me surgical masks, and dons one himself. The surgeon cuts me from neck to groin, a long, straight incision. Then he makes a cut at the top and another at the bottom, so that he can open me up like a box with flaps.

He starts poking around all over the place while my friend and I watch. I'm thinking that pretty soon he's going to be able to show me what I rather imagine is some little man, or specialized organ, or a magical stone or something that's the final repository for Fred. Only he can't find one. "Look under the liver," I suggest. He does, but finds nothing. "Behind my heart?" I ask. "I always heard the heart was our spiritual center." He can't find a thing, he sews me back up, leaving us both sadly disappointed.

"How about my head, Doc?" I ask him. "It always felt to me like *that's* where I really lived anyway. There's a sort of tingling behind my eyes, and now that I think about it, I'm pretty sure that's where I live. Can we try there?" He agrees. So, we rig up mirrors so that I can follow along, he hits me with a little more local anesthetic, and they open up my head with a saw in much the same way he opened up my torso. They stretch and peer in, and they bring the mirrors in close for me. "Do you see anything?" I ask. They both shake their heads no, and I have to confess that I can't see anything either.

"Of course your brain is still in there, but we can't mess with that," the surgeon says.

"But Doc, isn't that the most likely place for me to be? Surely I must be in the brain."

"That would be very scary work," he says.

"So what could happen?" I ask. "You can't paralyze me; there's nothing much left to paralyze. If you accidentally kill me, so be it. Let's give it a go."

The surgeon calls on his utmost skill and then actually begins to cut and probe into my brain. He hits parts of it that make my torso jerk. He hits other parts that bring up memories of my childhood. They are perfectly clear, like there's no age associated with them at all. When he touches another place, I can smell bacon frying! But try as he might, he can't unearth a Fred. "This is like cutting open a computer in search of the software," he says. "We know this body does stuff, but we can't see how. There is a lot of stuff in your head to process thoughts, but there's nothing here to *generate* them. There is no equivalent central *anything*.

"To tell you the truth," he says wistfully, "after looking at things from this point of view, I'm no longer sure this body even *runs* itself. It may be more like something akin to a robot, just a lot of sensors and such firing off all over the place. It's got certain hardwired attributes, and conditioning that it's gotten during its life. There are specific patterns we can identify, so we can say easily state that there is *Fredness* here, but that's as close as I can get to a real entity."

"Can you not think of *any* other solution?" I ask. "There's a lot at stake here."

"Don't I know it. I'm sorry, Fred," he says. "Or perhaps I should say, 'I'm sorry, *whoever or whatever it is that you are*.' Certainly there's a 'you' which exists in some form, because something's here that's watching this and talking to me. But my friend, so far as

I can tell there is no actual 'Fred' in there. I think that must be all made up. There's enough *space* for one, but that space seems to be uninhabited! In the end, 'Fred' appears to be merely an empty story, a fiction."

The man who made the bet leans over to me and says, "I don't think you've proven your case. I'm just about to call in my bet. For the last time, *where's Fred*?"

I don't have an answer for him. Do you?

*

CHAPTER FOUR
Step Four

PATTERNS

IN RECOVERY, THIS IS THE FIRST OF WHAT'S KNOWN AS THE "ACTION" steps. We use several columns on a sheet of paper to inventory our resentments, fears, and transgressions, including our sexual misconduct and peccadilloes. This last bit is always the most sensitive and secretive part of any fourth and fifth step combination (the fifth being when we share our fourth step findings). I had a recovery old timer who took hundreds of fifth steps over his life tell me that it was always some sex thing that people held back on most fiercely. That matches my experience.

Laying out the fourth step is a who-what-why sort of thing. We list who we've hurt, what happened, and why we did what we did, meaning what core motivation drove us: greed, lust, what have you. It can be a real eye opener, generally an unpleasant one, and it can be really helpful; I know it was for me. And the goal, of course, is abstinence and a more amicable life, which many find.

In Nonduality, however, we're not looking for defects of character, as is spoken of in recovery. Here we assume that all of this practical and valuable work has already been done, in one way or another, by the reader. This book is about the *next step*, but it doesn't suggest we skip the first twelve! Given that, let's look at the Nondual view.

If we start out in search of a problem, a problem is what we'll find. Here, we see that even the parts we don't like about ourselves or our world are still part of the entire *working*. From the absolute view, they are beyond good or bad. They *are*. This doesn't mean we deliberately overlook anything; quite the contrary. It means that as we begin to look at things a bit more dispassionately we'll see there's no need to *personalize* the world and its workings, and then crown it all with our judgments and opinions. Look at your hand when it's held up close to your eyes, and then continue to look at it as you slowly pull it back and away. This exercise is a good way of remembering that very often clarity comes with distance. This does not mean we are in any way distancing ourselves in terms of responsibility, interest, emotion, or compassion. First off, let me say that steps four through nine, at least as we view them through the eyes of Nonduality, are really somewhat arbitrary divisions of a single step: the movement toward embodying awakeness. We don't want to make this embodiment a goal, which would put it in an imaginary future, thus becoming a carrot before the donkey, but it's fine to go ahead and think of that as being the apparent process that's occurring. Even if you don't have any sense of awakening within yourself, rest assured that it's happening, but it's doing so in its own time. You wouldn't be reading these words if it wasn't happening on some level. But don't take too much comfort in that. It doesn't have to happen in *this* life. Without encouragement it probably won't.

We're going to be talking about digging into our patterns versus our past in these steps. Some patterns are efficient. We don't think about how to tie our shoes or drive a car. Those are patterns we learned a long time ago. We're no longer conscious of them when they work; it all happens by itself. Those patterns are efficient and helpful. The unconscious patterns we're going to be looking at in the next six chapters are also patterns of which we're not consciously aware. Most of them, however, are not helpful either to us, or our spiritual journey. In fact, much of the spiritual journey is actually coming to terms with these patterns. We begin to investigate patterns—ours and the collective patterns of the world—prior to awakening. Five years before I woke up I told my girlfriend, who's now my wife, "It's all about patterns. When realization comes, it will be about patterns." That's *all* I knew, but I sensed that very clearly. To a remarkable degree, I was intuitively correct.

I'll share another story with you. Some years back I was just beginning to get the feeling that I had gone as far as I could go by myself, and that I might need a real, live, flesh and blood teacher. Not everyone needs a teacher, but I did, and I suspect more people will benefit from having a teacher than not—by a considerable margin. It's clear that I didn't need direct aid to help me cross through the Gateless Gate, but I sure needed guidance in the new world I found once I was through it. I still do. And in relative retrospect, I wonder how much a teacher could have speeded up my arrival? I'm guessing quite a bit. The make-believe me's insistence on autonomy guaranteed the continued experience of duality.

Let's take a quick aside here on spiritual teachers, and then we'll come right back to our discussion of the fourth step.

It's funny how we feel about spiritual teachers. We think nothing of going to an auto specialist if our car goes on the blink. If we get ill, we turn to someone trained in the health field. We do the same for law, tax preparation, therapy, computers, art, education, and a thousand other areas. But when it comes to spirituality, the very field meant to unearth ego, what happens? After reading some books, maybe doing some meditation or inquiry, and perhaps delving into a little audio/video media, many people will do as I finally did, and seek out a living teacher. Of those who don't, most will fall into three camps. These camps are really patterns of resistance. They're worth taking a look at, and I'm guilty of having belonged to all of them at one time or another.

1. "I don't need a teacher. I'll do it my own way." I wonder how many seekers really know much at all about how to attain the enlightenment they're chasing? I'll hazard a guess and say that most seekers, just as I did, start out knowing zero. They're trying to lead themselves to a place they've never been.

2. "I don't trust teachers. They're probably all charlatans anyway." It simply isn't true. I knew nothing about awakening myself, and yet I made a sweeping, generally unfounded judgment that cut me off from anyone who might know more than I did.

3. "Spiritual teaching should be free." I've heard that a lot over the years. I happily paid my dentist, post carrier, landlord, cable guy, grocer, and everyone else who provided me a service. That's what spiritual teachers do; they provide a highly skilled service. Somehow I decided that spiritual teachers were the single exception, and that they should get their manna straight from God, and not through me.

My question for all of these positions is a simple one. Who wins if we're wrong? Ego. Our ego story has no investment in seeking skillful assistance to be rid of itself. It might be worth our looking at through the most open eyes we can muster.

Now let's get back to the story of my first experience with a living teacher. The teacher I felt closest to in that day was Adyashanti, although I'd never met him. I'd read all of his books and listened to a ton of audio. Well, Adya has an internet radio show once or twice a month, so I thought I'd try to reach him through that. Amazingly enough—or so it seemed to me—the first time I called him for help I got through to his screener in about thirty seconds, and I was the first caller on the show. As a general rule, I don't think it's quite that 1-2-3, but I should mention that it happened exactly the same way when I called a few weeks later to give him a follow-up report. The odds of that happening were 100%, just like they are with everything that happens, although they certainly *looked* considerably lower. Perhaps it really is true that when the student is ready the teacher will appear. Perhaps it can't be any other way.

I asked Adya how I could become a better servant of awareness. My question surprised him a little; it's not the usual sort of call he gets. I know that to be true, because he told me as much. He said that he'd once held a weekend intensive on that very topic and almost no one showed up for it, so he never did it again. Servant? Who wants to be a *servant*? Had the topic been how to be a better *master* of awareness, I suspect it would have been a real barnburner! In the discussion that followed that lead, Adya and I talked about the process of really getting down and examining the hard truth about ourselves. He referenced the fact that just as a lot of people were not lining up to be servants, not a whole lot of them were lining up to be searching and fearless about themselves either.

It was my turn to be surprised. "But Adya," I responded, "if I don't look at the dark, I'll never find the light." Whereupon he immediately, if metaphorically, stopped the show. His humility and generosity astonished me. "*That*," he said, "is the best spiritual teaching that's going to be heard on this or any other show tonight."

If we don't look at the dark, we'll never find the light. The fourth step, whether we're talking recovery, or Nonduality, is all about uncovering the truth about ourselves. Some of it's naturally going to be dark. We are human beings, and that means confused. Confused people do confused things. Only by seeing these things, and then seeing through them, are we able to get clear of that confusion and live in real harmony. We experience more peace, and so do those we come in contact with.

Living Nondually is not flatlining; quite the opposite. For example, I cry at the drop of a hat now. A sappy movie can bring forth a beautiful sort of innocent identification; I'm not looking for a cure for that. It's abundantly clear that I am far and away more helpful and useful to others than I have ever been. Everything matters. So let's be as clear as we can that at this stage in our spirituality we are simply looking for and dealing with unconscious patterns of unskillful behaviors—patterns that can be harmful to others, ourselves, and our so-called spiritual development. Our goal here is far-reaching—liberation from the yoke of the *myth* of separation.

As seen here, these impersonal patterns we investigate don't actually belong to anyone. They arise spontaneously and simply *happen*—over and over again, with absolutely no one at the wheel. This "no one at the wheel" is why, at this level, personalization will hinder us. We can choose to view these patterns as our very own tragic flaws, or we can choose to investigate unconscious and unskillful patterns, but we can't do both. Once we own such a thing, it immediately becomes "my problem, which I need to fix." As soon as that occurs, we've already lost the battle simply by making it a battle. It needs to be clearly seen that ego is behind both assumptions! It can't help but win. Whether this supposed "I" fixes the problem, or fails to fix the problem, the "I" remains, and with it, suffering.

Granted, we can certainly see that actions happen *through* an apparent "us," so the body-mind is squarely responsible. There's no sloughing that responsibility off with grand-sounding absolutist avoidance statements. Our body-mind, meaning the flesh suit being worn by who we *think* we are prior to awakening, is indeed the responsible tool, awake or not. However, we have already said that what appears to be "our" body-mind is not really "us." Just because it exists doesn't automatically make it ours. A man takes his suit off in the evening and hangs it in the closet; he doesn't go stand in there until morning. The suit is not *him*, and he knows it; he is not confusing the two. He puts it on and he takes it off. We, however, presume we *are* our flesh suits, at least until we inquire our way out of that presumption. The lights are on in every sentient body, be it human, squirrel, or lily, but there's no one home in any of them. There is no separate entity anywhere outside of our heads. We are not living our lives. We are *being lived*. There is just one life, and all there is, is *livingness*.

Our human unit gets propelled, bumped, jolted, and flipped just like a steel ball in a pinball machine. The difference with us is that after the round is over we come in *behind the action* and retroactively take credit or blame for the whole game, for all events and situations. None can escape our vigilance! We announce that we won or we lost after every move, and in the overall result as well, thus taking upon ourselves the mantle of perpetrator, or victim, or both. Meanwhile, we self-righteously assign guilt or innocence to any and all with careless abandon. We assert that we, the pinballs and stars of the show, have free will. Furthermore, we say, our enemies—which means anyone I don't like—have control over their actions as well. Everyone, me-you-them, is nicely set up for guilt. This makes as much sense as endowing a hammer with volition because it hits one nail and not another.

This difference in approach, whether it's a personal world or a neutral one, and where I assign volition, has quite large ramifications. The difference between an *activity* and an *entity* is the difference between responsibility and guilt. The two negative emotions that do no one any good are guilt and shame, and they are both birthed in this notion of free will. Based on an entirely erroneous core conclusion, we mercilessly assign devious plots and plans to ourselves and others. This allows us to foster self-hatred and resentments, and to indefinitely remain in resistance to *what is*. Let us remember that on a relative level, *what is* is always the product of "what was." When we accept or resist the present moment, then by definition we are simultaneously accepting or resisting all that apparently came before. It's good to note that we cannot *actually* reject the present moment. *It already is.* We can't reject a rainy day when it's already raining. We can *resist* it, which will affect our mental state, a state which then ripples outward, but we can't undo a single moment, or unring a single bell. The now always *is*, precisely *as it is*, regardless of our opinion of it.

We can accomplish all we need to accomplish without designating or assigning either blame or innocence. There has to be an entity involved for either one of those to make any sense. In the absence of a personal entity—ours or our enemy's—how can such judgment take place, and do guilt and shame even have a role? We know from practical experience that guilt and shame will ultimately *fuel* the scrutinized behavior into a closed feedback-response loop. Once we're in such a loop, it's virtually impossible to get off of it on our own. That why we couldn't kick our addictions. There was no such thing as off-the-ride so long as our only reference was ourselves.

This is the chief reason we see specific negative patterns emerge and continue through generations of families. *You can't see through what you can't see.* If all of your mirrors are showing you the same sorts of images, you have no dissident reference point. That goes on indefinitely until somehow a break in the chain develops. A single individual wakes up to at least *that* specific damaging behavior. They could now be said to be *enlightened* to that behavior. They see things as they are, and the stories begin to unravel.

The guilt/shame/blame closed feedback loop is also a key part of why there is so much recidivism in behavioral addictions, and relapse in substance addictions. Gaining enough clarity, even temporarily, to quit responding to cravings, is so radical, and apparently random, that we generally ascribe it to grace. I'll offer no argument against that assessment. It is as predictable as lightning, and cares nothing whatsoever about apparent worthiness, or the lack of it. However, the real key to our success, be it ridding ourselves of the chains of addiction, or adequately penetrating patterns, is in what comes next.

We have to *stay awake* to the confusion.

How we view what came before our moment of freeing clarity-by-grace, and how we view what comes afterward, is going to be the measure of our serenity, and probably the measure of our success. Shame and guilt stimulate a lot of stress, and the only thing that has the power to relieve that stress is the very substance or behavior we're ashamed and guilty about. Finding an unconscious pattern in ourselves and then indignantly railing about it is itself another unconscious pattern. Ego has once again come in the back door to curse itself through the front. It then backs up and laughs itself silly in the hallway between the two doors. Guilt and shame are the sandman's tools, and you can bet they'll put us back to sleep.

So, our unclinging approach to "the hard truths about ourselves" is key. Our goal here is nothing short of the *literal* liberation from the bondage of self. If we neither go into nor take on a sense of personal, entity-based ownership, then our entry, cataloging, and eventual exit from the process will be cleaner, clearer, and more

effective. We are coming to grips with the patterns and ramifications of "what was," so that they can be brought to the light and
dispelled. If we cut a light on in a dark room, we don't then have
to get a broom and sweep out the darkness. The presence of light is
enough to bring about an absence of darkness. But we have to hit
every corner.

This discovery process, like a recovery inventory, is best
approached thoughtfully, and actually written out, pen to paper.
Putting things into writing via our own hand is critical. There's
less slither room when we do it this way, and we can use all the
insurance we can get. Yet let's not make a list, unless we can call one
thing on a sheet of paper a "list." How many things can we really
work on at once? One. Our mind, however smoothly and speed-
ily, is always firing on a single cylinder at a time. So let's pick just
one unconscious pattern and see if we can pierce it. It's no longer
entirely unconscious, or we couldn't even identify it. As recovery
literature tells us, however, "self-knowledge" is not enough. What
we are after here is *Self*-knowledge. Most often we come to know
what is true by exposing what is false. Earnest seekers will embrace
this process; the faint-hearted will fall back into denial—until they
don't. And don't worry about the confusion patterns you're leaving
behind for the moment. Better we focus on one at a time. The others
aren't going anywhere; we can come back, and back, and back.

We can think of these unconscious patterns as being like balloons. In a metaphoric sense, they are self-contained bubbles simply
floating around in spaciousness. For the moment we'll call that spaciousness "mind." We find that these balloons behave like magnets.
We find ourselves attracted to one balloon, while another one gets
pushed away, as if blocked by a magnetic force field. We love to get
up on a pedestal and decry the behaviors of others while trumpet-
ing our own (at least the ones we're proud of), but there's much,
much more at play here than a mere sense of morality or fairness.
We could say with some degree of accuracy that the movement of
the entire universe is behind even the crossing of our legs. That
sounds preposterous, but Jesus tells us that "every hair of your head

has been counted." The sheer *detail* of the dream we call the world is staggering. And every bit of it is already registered within who you really are. It's all intimately connected. Here's a lovely paradox: nothing is happening by accident, and nothing is happening by design. The one thing going on encompasses, but is beyond, both ends of that duality. It's all unfolding just like origami: we can see one surface at a time. The mind cannot contain this; it can only lead us to the cliff that grace then invites us to leap from.

One piece of good news is that, with a smattering of clarity and a boatload of willingness, we can, in fact, indirectly *influence* our dream character's apparent spiritual development—and actions related to that development. We appear to do this from within the dream itself, when we take our stand as awareness itself. Enlightenment allows for an experience of something similar to "lucid dreaming," only it's within what we call the waking state of everyday life. The movement between waking and sleep is the movement between one dream and another. Only in deep sleep do we let go of dreaming—and in between every thought! Let me be clear, however, that at no point is the dream character itself affecting real events. The character, as a separate, volitional entity, simply doesn't exist. The dream character is apparently affecting dream events related to clarity. We're back to paradox, and it's a place we might as well get comfortable being in if we're going to go very far in our understanding.

We want to again remind ourselves that this idea is not suggestive of any sort of direct, intentional control, or manifestation, of dream-world events or conditions. We should be clear that such practices are directed by and for ego. They occur in the dream for the dream character. That doesn't make them bad or wrong; this is not a debate on that topic. As it's seen here, however, "mental manifestation" is highly likely to pull our attention away from getting off the dream wheel altogether. That doesn't mean we have to renounce either the body's comfort, or its apparent security, but it does mean keeping our eyes and our energy directed toward truth and not appearance.

We can "know" our true nature, by which I mean we can be operating from a fairly developed state, and still exhibit quite poor patterns of behavior. We do what we do until we do something else, just as a fan continues to turn for awhile even after it's unplugged. It's neither accurate nor appropriate to write off those behaviors because it's been seen in some moment of absolute vision that there's "nothing to do, and no one to do it." At that point, ego is using the teaching itself to hunker back into caustic blindness. We're convinced we're awake and advanced, but the funny thing is, all the rest of the world thinks we're an asshole. In the long run, however, that apparent stasis is going to end up being temporary. Ultimately our tent has to be pitched in one camp or the other: within conscious awakeness, or within the dream of an entity, even if that entity is declaring it doesn't exist. Piercing unconscious patterns is the act of hammering down our tent pegs in the camp of conscious awakeness.

If we can thoroughly pierce our patterns, many of them will begin to deflate and finally disappear on their own. In my experience, some either don't fade, or they take quite a while to do it. Either way, we can be free of them being *ours*. That alone is amazingly freeing. We may have a lot more blind patterns than we think. Attempting to force them away is in fact feeding them. We are not held back in this process so much by an inability to see the truth as we are by an unwillingness to accept it. Here is where the judgments play such a large role.

Look at our track record with addiction. How well did we do fighting addiction? Most of us didn't do very well, or we wouldn't have found ourselves in recovery. We won't do any better trying to *conquer* patterns. In this case, as in addiction, all we can do is surrender our patterns to the light. Perhaps they can be undone, *but not by "us."* Our part, as I see it, is the willingness to *be changed.* If the pattern itself isn't changed or modified, then our part is to accept that this is how things are—until they aren't. Either way, we've not dismissed them, but neither are we actively suffering from them in a psychological way. The body is responsible, but I am not left feeling guilty, shamed, or disconnected from society. I am not blaming anyone. I am in an optimal position for healing to take place.

Everything already *is*. Surrender is the actionless act of granting permission for the world to be as it *already* is. It's simply a way of dropping the personalized "me." This allowing lowers or removes our shields, which are not in the least effective in keeping anything *out*, but they are wonderful at keeping things *in*. Everything is now free to come and go; nothing is stuck. In the absence of an attic, there is no trapped ghost.

So we take a sheet of paper and write down one pattern we want to see through. One is plenty. Put the paper safely aside somewhere. It'll be several chapters before we're ready to use it, because the fifth step in recovery—sharing our list with our Higher Power and another human being—is not the method we'll use in Nonduality. In recovery we're trying to effect change in the relative world. The fourth step is a great strategy for doing that. Here, however, we're just trying to discover truth while we allow the relative world to do what it does.

Now, if you want to write down two or twenty or two hundred patterns you want to write through while you're doing this, fine. But use two or twenty or two hundred pieces of paper. This one-thing-at-a-time focus is sort of like recovery's one-day-at-a-time slogan. Using this breaks our patterns down into smaller sized segments that reveal a larger truth. I'm sure you know how to eat an elephant: one bite at a time.

We need to understand more about our true nature before we go on to deal with these patterns, which is why that comes later in this text than it does in recovery. In recovery I always told people, "You can't fix what you can't see." The steps are great at helping us learn to see-and-fix.

Here, it's perhaps more true to say, "You can't see from a fixed position." In other words, there is no such thing as seeing truth from an egoic center. The fixed position of me-ness is what distorts reality to begin with. We can take another step in the direction of self-discovery through the exercise below. This is not something you do just once. It's fast and easy, and instantly effective. I still use it, and others report using it many times a day. It's a great way to stay out of your head and your body, meaning out of your imagination and into real life.

This exercise is designed to help us begin to see what's real and what's imaginary. Most of what we experience is our imagination. It, too, chiefly consists of patterns. Once again we're going to use me as the subject, but once you've read the exercise, substitute yourself. It's always tempting to jump past these exercises. I know, I used to do it, too. Yet when I started actually following the directions in the books, instead of running ahead for *more information* that might "get me there," then I started making real progress. I'm confident it'll be the same for you.

Excercise 4: The Photographer

*

One morning I was sitting in my chair in my tiny living room, where I go to read and meditate in the mornings. On this morning, however, something had happened. I forget what it was, but it probably had something to do with my book business, because I was righteously steamed, and it was too early for me to have talked to anyone. Oh, the power of email.

This anger was unusual for me, and so I gave it my attention. This is how we learn. I took a close look at this anger in the way a father would look at a spoiled, whining child. It was silly, this railing against what already was, and of course as soon as I became aware of it, I knew that it was not *my* anger; it was just an anger *pattern*, one of the telling patterns of *Fredness*. I'd found a situation I was not awake to. Under scrutiny and acceptance, however, it dropped, because in the absence of resistance—even if it's internal—there's nothing to bind it.

Suddenly I thought about what a photographer would see if one looked in my front window. What they would have seen on that morning was a pleasant looking, calm man in a comfortable chair, within an artfully decorated and pleasing room, holding a book and having a cup of hot tea. If the photographer took a picture of the scene and then looked at the digital image on his camera, that's exactly what he would see: man, chair, room, book, and tea.

The photographer would be unable to see the storm in my head. This is because the storm in my head *wasn't real*. I had made it up. I was having a war in my head, with (marginally) raised blood pressure, harder than normal breathing, and perhaps even a touch of a the angry shakes; I don't remember the details. But there I was, sitting there in a world of peace and beauty suffering all the wounds of heated battle, and yet there was *no actual war* going on! I was suffering purely from my own imagination. I was under no threat, was taking no insult; everything was peaceful and lovely. It was the kind of picture you might see in an ad for insurance or something, where they're trying to sell you a sense of well-being, security and accord.

The only thing any photographer can ever take a picture of is reality. What was reality on that morning? Man, chair, room, book, tea. Whether I thought about them or not, those five things would still exist. If I forgot to think about my war, however, it would cease to exist, thus it clearly wasn't real to begin with. That's the acid test to see if something is real or not. Is it still there when you don't think about it? If not, it's not real. My war was one of thoughts, and only thoughts. Once I gave them permission to play out, they petered out instead.

Try this the next time you catch your mind going nuts on you. Think about a photographer—what would they see in their oh-so-objective lens? Their lens can't hear the constant complaining of the commentator in your head. (In the rooms they sometimes call that voice "the shitty committee!") Their lens won't show what's wrong with the world, because their lens can't see *what isn't*. Their lens won't show how the world should be, because it can only focus on *what is.* Man, chair, room, book, and tea. There's nothing to suffer about in that. And there is zero evidence that it should be any way other than it is.

*

While we're on this subject of reality versus thinking, let's take it a step further.

Our photographer couldn't take a picture of a Fred, either. He could take a picture of the human being sitting in the chair, but not of Fred, because the Fred part exists only in our heads. It may be the product of a collective agreement, but it is certainly no more than that. You call, "Hey, Fred!" and I turn my head. That's our agreement. But that doesn't make me an actual Fred, whatever that is. It makes me something that *answers to the name* Fred. That doesn't make "Fred" real. We can collectively agree that the moon should be made of cheese, but that doesn't make it so.

However, there is another set of collective agreements present that carries with it the stamp of truth. The product of those agreements was what the camera *could actually see.* There was a man in the room of a certain size, shape, and age, with certain distinguishing features. But that's not a Fred. What is the reality there? Man, shortish, average build, silver hair, and glasses. There's nothing *personal* there. It's a collection of objects. If the photographer got stung by a bee and momentarily forgot all about what was in that room, when he came back to it, nothing would have disappeared. Everything would still be there, because everything is, for our purposes here, *real.*

Everything personal, however, is made up. It's pure fiction. It's all in my head. If you brought in a stranger and didn't tell them my name, they wouldn't be able to guess it. They wouldn't know that things weren't going my way, and that the world was out of whack. All of that is my imagination chewing on itself and driving itself crazy. If the photographer hung around long enough he'd see the man repeatedly doing certain things in certain ways. He could change the setting to video, and record specific patterns. He could show those patterns to someone else, and they'd know right away what they were. Man feeding birds. Man typing. Man petting cats. Man reading. (I didn't say they were *exciting* patterns!) The patterns are always simple. The stories *about* the patterns are where the complexity lies.

Now, if you and I want to call those specific patterns *Fredness*, which speaks to their verb-like qualities, that's close enough to the truth to *call it* truth for now. It's truth with a convenient handle. But Fred? He doesn't exist. How can we be sure? Because every time I get involved with something else, I forget him and he ceases to exist. A man continues to type, and there is typing, but there's no Fred doing it. It's just a pattern, firing away onto a keyboard. The mind is too intent on the story it's telling about the livingness going on to give a damn who's telling it. *So it drops the identity.*

The same thing happens between every thought. No thinking? No Fred. It does the same thing in deep sleep. No thinking or dreaming? No Fred. Granted, when the thinking cranks back up, even when the dreaming cranks back up, there will be again be misidentification with some specific body-mind. But in the absence of those, there is just the one thing going on. Lots of Fredness, but not a Fred to be found anywhere.

CHAPTER FIVE
Step Five

CLARITY

IN THE RECOVERY TRADITION, WE TAKE OUR FIFTH STEP WITH A trusted spiritual adviser who has promised confidentiality. We bring our written inventory and sit down with our adviser to explore truth. I've helped people work quite a few fifth steps over the years. The idea, as I saw it, was to introduce insight into history, and clarity into confusion. I always offered up illustrations of my own past to make the other person comfortable, and to share what I had learned. Once they'd heard something of my story, they could pretty well spill the beans about their own pasts in complete comfort. I never heard a fifth step any worse than my own, though I heard a couple that bore very strong parallels.

In a way, *all* fifth steps are the same, because they all point to our innate selfishness. Only the details differ; the overall pattern is always identical. I say "innate selfishness," because self-interest doesn't spring from a personal me; a personal me springs from self-interest. In the absence of self-interest, show me a personal me. I don't think you can. Selfishness is a real, live, ongoing relative pattern. There's nothing real about ego; it's invented and reinvented on a moment-to-moment basis. This is why the ego is impossible to fix: you can't polish what isn't there to begin with.

That's how we can tell if we're making headway toward truth. If our fifth step is not pointing us toward selfishness, we might want to do some serious personal inquiry and then start over.

Familiar patterns of conditioning arise within similar circumstances. Once you've heard a few fifth steps you have heard them all. You could map the patterns; I guess psychologists do this all the time. As a layman, what I know is that bringing these patterns to light is miraculous. I'm not going to argue over whether we fix them, or they are fixed for us, because I think that's another free will/destiny argument. I can tell you that things change when you go through this process. I never took a legitimate fifth step that went poorly, and I never listened to one that didn't help me as much as it helped the other guy. Confession has a long history, and it's easy to see why. It works. Here, however, this step is seen quite differently.

In the Nondual tradition, our goal in these "action steps," as they are known in the rooms, is not to clean up the "wreckage of our past," but to clean up the cloudiness of our present. Just like in the recovery fifth step, we are bringing clarity to confusion—but we are our own sponsor, and the confusion we're dealing with is also our own. This is something that we not only *can* do alone, but it is something that ultimately we *must* do alone. All we really need is the courage to be rigorously honest, but that's like saying all we need to breathe is air. There's nothing to that exercise if you've got plenty of oxygen, but it's a damn steep hill to climb if you don't.

For many of us who arrive at this place, the motivation is identical to what drove us into recovery to begin with. Our old friends, still thriving pockets of misery and disillusionment, now experienced within recovery, are what we needed to prompt us to look abroad for help. For others, there is still a feeling of incompleteness, and a deep spiritual hunger has developed. We want to see just how far this train can take us. Frankly, by the time we arrive at this stage, most of us have had lots of *both* misery and hunger. What matters is that we're here, and we're ready to dig deep and explore this sack of conditioning that's wandering the earth.

Before we go on, let's remember that our overall goal here, quite counter-intuitively, is not to attempt to directly get rid of a specific behavior, or to try and change our character's makeup. We can think of our body-mind, that which we think we are, as a character in a play. That's fairly true, though not absolutely true. It'll do for our present understanding.

Other than exactly how things already are, we don't have any notion of how they "should be." This "should be" is simply another word for *what isn't*. We are determined to live in *what is*. Our purpose for all of these steps is simply to experientially find out the truth about ourselves. That alone is the game changer. We don't know what we're "supposed" to be like, other than what we *are* like; or what we're "supposed" to be doing, other than what we are *already* doing. We do know that we don't want to be in opposition to what is already happening. We're surrendered to all that is, *as it is*.

If upon our offering our "will and our lives" up to the light of conscious scrutiny brings about what we see as appropriate change, great. It has certainly been that way with me, however slow. And I know it has been that way with many others I've spoken to and corresponded with. If it doesn't, we can rest easily that things are exactly as they're supposed to be until they aren't. We're not hiding out in the absolute playing the no-responsibility game, and we're not vehemently declaring that we should be different, and that by golly and God, we're *going* to be different! It didn't work with our addiction, and it won't work our other objectionable patterns. This is not a defeatist attitude; not by a longshot. It's surrender. We're right back at the first four words of the first step: "Admitted we were powerless." We have to remember to carry those words with us through every step. We're just giving this thing our best; that's all. And all we're trying to do is discover the truth, not alter it.

Regardless of any direct result, or a lack thereof, or what timetable any result might be on, we'll have done our part. *What is* includes *us*. If coming to terms with the way things are is what we're out to do, then there's no sense in our harboring hurtful opinions about our inadequate selves. We are perfectly adequate at every moment. We are always meeting our challenges perfectly, even when we meet them with apparent failure. How we are is how we are—*until we're not*.

Arguing that we should be otherwise won't change *what is*, and we'll suffer for our poorly chosen beliefs, opinions, and positions. Bringing our ongoing patterns to the light of awareness, and acknowledging the truth, is enough. If we are consistent, change or no change, compulsive self-criticism and self-congratulation will begin to fade, along with second-guessing ourselves, and living in the nagging fear that we didn't "do it right," *whatever* it was that we did.

Let's take a look at a way of seeing that could help us transcend the simple boundaries of right and wrong, and the presence or absence of personal volition. We're *not* saying, "If it feels good, do it." Truth is far more subtle than that. What we are saying is closer to, "If it feels *right*, do it." We'd want to check with our heart on matters of ethics, not our brain, which often has vacation homes in our wallets and loins.

Excercise 5: A Way of Seeing

✳

Let me share a way of seeing with you.

Use your imagination for a moment and think of your body-mind as a pure sensing organism, something akin to a skin-clad robot, with cameras for eyes, and having all the other sensing instruments built into it, too. Other than sight, this robot can pass along hearing, feeling, touching, smelling, and even thoughts. Granted, this is all a bit crude. Nonetheless, in the spirit of inquiry and just for now, pretend that your body-mind is a way for consciousness to experience what's happening in a certain neighborhood of its very own dream. In this mental exercise, you are essentially a mobile computer, with the ability to process loads of information and ideas, but without the capacity to generate anything original.

In its neighborhood, in its apparently quite finite locale, let's think of your sensing organism as being a virtual hand and eye of God. In its passive and pure sensing way it looks out upon the world of objects and *relays* what it senses "on up the line," so to speak. We could say it issues nonstop *uploads*. In truth, of course, your sensing mechanism body-mind is an object just like all of the objects it's recording and passing along. This is where it gets confusing.

Since your body-mind is the thing apparently *doing* the recording, *since it can't see itself seeing*, it quickly loses all sense of its own objectivity. This is important, so let me repeat it in slightly different words. *The eye can't see itself*, by which I mean, the sensing unit can't put the camera behind itself, and thus witness itself as an object, even though this is clearly the case. It begins to think it's uploading to *itself*. It believes itself to be the *subject* of and lord over the world of objects, the sovereign of all it surveys, and it surveys *everything*. And given its point of view, where the world seems to expand outward from the starting point of the eyes or just behind them, it believes it has *evidence* of its "subjective supremacy." The mind will *always* find evidence to support its beliefs. In this case what we have is a glove confusing itself as a hand; an outfit that believes itself to be the outfitter.

The sensing unit feels like it's an active *part* of the story. It thinks it's *in* the story instead of just recording it. What a confusing case of mistaken identity! What a hoot! And of course that unit *is* in the story, but it's one more *object* in a story chock full of objects, objects that all apparently arise to an unseen watcher.

Imagine now that my body is also a sensing organism, and I'm in the story you're witnessing. You can still call me Fred if you want to, although I know that there's only Fredness here. There is specific, patterned activity by the so-called Fred sensing unit that one could *confuse* as being an entity that has the free will to choose and direct all those patterns, but that's not really the case. There's no entity here. The Fred pattern is an empty suit firing this pattern and that when conditioning meets circumstance. It's part of what's spontaneously happening in a *world* that's spontaneously happening. In fact, it is not *other than* the world. It is part and parcel of it.

The only difference between my unit and yours is that my unit is not as clouded as it once was. It is not a special somebody. It's a totally ordinary bit of equipment without much in the way of a sense of self, though there are still some cirrus clouds about. Now, my unit can't actually be *aware* of the dream it's in, because in this exercise, it's a living, yet essentially empty box! We could, however, say my unit is very nearly *transparent*. As a result of that ordinariness, that transparency, the consciousness behind the box, as it were, can see straight through to the dream and *know it's a dream*!

You are dreaming that a separate, secluded body-mind is living a separate, secluded life. In contrast to that, I—I am speaking here as consciousness, not as Fredness—I clearly *see*, in real-time, not just in memory, that the body-mind I feel most associated with is just a big, complex set of sensors. I haven't forgotten who I actually am. I know that my skin-clad sensing device is part of the objective world; that it, too, is an object among objects. It's not even a *special* object—there are *billions* of these things on this *one planet* in the outback of the outskirts of the universe!

And every single one of those seven billion units thinks they are the subject to a world of objects, the sovereign of all they survey. Rather than delve into all that just now, let's get on with our mental exercise.

Our two units start a conversation and I—the Fred unit—share what I know with your unit. In other words, consciousness is talking *through* a clear unit (that is itself, since there's just once thing going on) *to* an unclear unit that is also itself. You could say it's God talking to God about God! I tell the part of me that's confused, the part behind your unit, everything that it's forgotten. Thinking that you're still a unit, you can't believe it; it doesn't make a bit of sense. Nonsense and bother! Nothing I say can convince you of the truth. Suddenly something snaps. The hooks that held the clouds in place let loose, the clouds disappear, and suddenly your unit is transparent, too! You, consciousness, that which fills and powers the entire universe thought you were a little human being! How funny is THAT? You were playing a big joke on yourself, and you bought it hook, line, and sinker! Oh joyous joy! Oh wondrous wonder! It is *instantly* seen that you are without center or circumference, without beginning or end, without limitation in any way. It is instant, because this seeing actually takes place out of time. The dream of time is over. The dream of space is over. There you are, your radiant, magnificent self, beyond time, beyond space, beyond any concept of any kind. *And you were there all along*!

There is laughter, endless, boundless laughter as the worlds shake and the suns shiver. Nothing was ever so funny as this.

This allegory is very close to the truth. Mind you, it's *not* the truth but I think it's fair to say it's really close. Regardless, this is a good place to remind ourselves about fingers, moons, and provisional truths.

Now that we are out of that story, let me ask you a question. When the error of misidentification is cleared up, *who* is it that saw through it? Does the sensing organism "wake up"? How could it? It's neither asleep, nor awake, and never could be. It's just a passive object, entirely animated and used as a handy dandy tool by the only true subject—the one thing going on. Only the one thing going on can see itself, or fail to see itself. The sensing unit is not suddenly enlightened. *Nobody is*! Nobody needs to be! The animating presence has never been asleep; it was confused, so to speak, in that location—and untold others. Now that it's no longer confused at that pinpoint, it begins *to live that organism* in a different way. For the sake of clarity in language— and *only* for clarity within the dream between dream objects—we now say that the organism in "your" location, what you may still—or again—think of as "your" body-mind, is "enlightened." *But it's just a way of speaking about a way of seeing.* Nothing has actually happened beyond a recognition.

Nothing was added, and nothing was lost. Nothing was taught, and nothing was learned. The one thing going on is always already complete. This is what is known. *To itself.*

The first movement here is often a 180. We see what we are not. We are not the little human, we are consciousness. But if we keep on clearing our windshield, then with grace we will discover that we are beyond that limitation, too. There is only one thing going on, which means it must *include* our humanness. We are not *either* divinity or humanity. We are both divinity *and* humanity. We are the whole thing. Now we know not just what we aren't, but also what we really are. We see our face everywhere we look. We now have a foot in each world. This is the complete 360, the full opening to reality.

Now we have to learn how to live this truth, *as* this truth. This is why each one of these steps is so important, so vital. With our hearts firmly planted in heaven, and our feet firmly planted on earth, we find it very helpful to continue clearing up our body-mind's apparent cloudiness, no matter at what stage of the spiritual process we may find ourselves. As a very wise friend of mine told me, this path is like a dictionary, where we go from word to word to word, simply for the sake of the adventure, learning at every step, and moving on and on, without hope or need of an end-point. But we have to do it by ourselves, because it is now seen that there is no one else to turn to. *We are it*. This is it. Knowing this absolute truth, yet fully honoring the relative world, we move on to the next step.

CHAPTER SIX
Step Six

UNDERSTANDING

WITH THIS STEP IN THE RECOVERY TRADITION, IT IS OUR JOB, AS THE step is worded, to become "entirely ready to have God remove our defects of character." I completely appreciate how this step is seen and used in the recovery environment. This step, in combination with the others, can provide a release from the terror and waste that is addiction. Few achievements, whether individual or institutional, can rival that one. It's sort of the action side of surrender. It's a personal *statement* that "we can't do it," not just a hastily adopted position.

From our in-the-world, relative viewpoint, all of us have led flawed lives. All of us have been unkind, selfish, even mean. Some of us have done terrible things. Others of us have done things that others might not deem to be so terrible, but which we do. The internal measure of sin, if you will, is always a personal one. Thus what one person might think to be a fairly minimal affair is completely eating the lunch—and the serenity—of another. What matters here is what is it that's bothering *us*? We don't want to unnecessarily beat ourselves up, and we don't want to turn our eyes away. What we want is real understanding prior to our taking the step. There's no point in asking a Higher Power to take away what we ourselves have not seen and understood.

In Nonduality, as ever, things are seen rather differently. From this view, when we take our stand as awareness, we see that no one is living "their life." *We are being lived* as part of the one thing that's going on. It would really be more accurate to say that life is simply living. There's no us separate from that living. However, how the we we-think-we-are is lived seems to be at least partially contingent on where we've taken our stand. Where we're seeing from changes what we see, and what we see in large part determines how these bodies respond.

I will leave it to other, brighter stars than I to explain all of this theory for you some day. I can't. I can intuit much of this, but I can't explain it, and there's some that I can't even intuit. What I do know is *what works*. So I am telling you that if you take this wheeled box and move it back and forth across your lawn, at the end of the day your grass will be shorter. Do you want to know how the lawn mower works, or do you want short grass?

I appreciate that we feel like it has to be one way or the other. That's the classic 180 paradox. Whichever side yo u choose is wrong, because a true answer is always an inclusive answer. Still, the brain nearly insists that we hold one way as truth. There is another splendid example of these kinds of co-existing truths that we'll touch on just to remind our ranting brains that something like this really *is* possible.

Without going back into it, let's gently remind ourselves of the comparison of classical and quantum mechanics that we went over in the introduction to this book. We saw that two different sets of rules can apply to two different circumstances found in a single, common world, all without one side negating the truth, need, or effectiveness of the other. Leaving the science metaphor behind us, let's look at this in a bit broader way before we continue with this step.

This idea of harmony, of two different outstretched arms coming together to create a mutual inclusiveness, is found throughout Nonduality as it's being presented here. We are everything, while simultaneously we are no-thing. We are both human and divine. We have one foot in the absolute, and the other in the relative. None of these double positions are at odds with each other. They are like fraternal twins. We've talked some about "spiritual 180's," where in the light of a new truth, an old truth is dropped. This is a logical sequence of events, but it's not always the one that bears the most fruit. In fact, this natural selection and progression are nearly always incomplete.

Where the brain loves a world of on and off, zero and one, black and white, the universe itself is neither so simple, nor so divisive. We have only to look around us. I may think vanilla ice cream is the best, while you believe it's chocolate. If we just check in with reality we'll see that we're not limited to choosing only one or the other. Both are already here, along with a plethora of other choices. It's a Ben & Jerry's world. You and I can both be "right" in a limited way. Anytime the belief in one thing demands the complete negation of a second, we should probably take a good look at that first belief. It's almost surely a 180, meaning it's not an accurate model by which to steer our path.

This is the kind of thing we just want to notice, but notice *clearly*. And that noticing doesn't rule out our taking a 180 jump in a conditional way. It may be an important jump for us, a big move forward, but let's not confuse it with the truth. Living truth is the process of staying open to *new* truth, and not giving into the ego's desire to land. Reality is ever-fresh. If we look at a hard position's opposite, we'll find the other side of the equation decrying ours as being untrue. If we can at least conditionally accept both sides of a thing, allowing them to coexist on their own terms—leaving ample room for doubt and uncertainty, we are likely to have our feet set really close to the truth.

When we allow a measure of uncertainty we are simply sticking with the facts. Things *are* uncertain. What do we really know? Even in the academic disciplines, truth is up for grabs. We can speak of scientific or historical facts, for instance, but as time progresses both science and history change their beliefs, opinions, and positions, and get rewritten. That's a clear statement that their "facts" remain unstable and adjustable, which is highly laudable. They, too, must remain open to a measure of uncertainty. If trained scientists and historians don't know what's really going on in their own fields, in fields where everything appears so cut and dried, where does that leave *us*? In the same boat, I think, and up the very same creek. Let's allow what already is to be: uncertainty is part of reality. *Loose* is good.

Without a mountain of fixed positions on every subject, divergent arisings can coexist, and often we find they complement each other more than they contradict each other. If we can begin to introduce this more inclusive, holistic thinking into more and more areas of our lives, we'll find that it does two things almost immediately. It brings peace to the present, and it introduces what can become a growing—and freeing!—doubt about the validity of an extreme position—*any* extreme position. If we can begin to relinquish our attachment to "having it all *right*," we can start to enjoy the rewards of "having it all."

In chapter five we discussed the fact that we don't actually know what we're supposed be "rid of," if anything. We are beginning to sense that we're certainly not supposed to be rid of anything until we actually *are* rid of it. This approach brings us into alignment with actual reality as it's playing out—unless or until it changes. This is the ever-simple message of reality: *things are as they are.* Any position, any center, is wholly imaginary. To defend or promote an imaginary world is to live in insanity. I know I've said almost that very same thing before. I'll be saying it again, too. Repetition is a key tool of spiritual discovery. As our own condition changes, then what we get from the same phrase changes as well.

If something about us needs to be modified, it will be—exactly when it's supposed to be. Our great choice, the choice that makes all the difference, is to take our stand in awareness *right now*, and thus not duplicate those unskillful patterns while new ones spontaneously develop. Patterns change to fit what is seen, and what is seen changes as our stand changes.

As we talked about in chapter four, our body-minds are responsible, but we haven't said that the things they are responsible for were or are, in an *absolute* sense, "wrong." The universe isn't in the habit of making mistakes, or explaining itself to the likes of us. Wrong, as we have already seen, is simply a judgment based on a relative, ephemeral location. Points of view, like reactions, arise spontaneously from seemingly random intersections of conditioning and circumstance. There's nothing inherently true in any of them, nor do they require an owner. They arise and fall on their own, without our help, and without need of our either taking on or projecting guilt, shame, or blame. Everyone's trying to do their best, although most of us are very confused, and some of us are tragically confused. Let's at least try to accept reality, which is that these units do what they do until they do something else. The lights are on, but there's no one home.

And here's a news flash: the past is *over*. What happened, happened, and *what is*, is. Truth is always *what is*, and it's always right here in front of our noses. Our job, if we accept it—our single choice—is to witness reality from the clearest point available. That point is found wherever a human being takes its stand as awareness. Awake or asleep, our actions are guided more by subtle feelings, and responses or reactions to conditioned arisings, than they are by any sort of decisive thinking. Indeed, most of the time sleeping body-minds are working in some unconscious closed pattern, and there's no natural opportunity for anything new to ever occur. Whether the circles of our patterns are large or small, sleeping body-minds are typically set in a default position, blindly doing the same thing over and over again.

How many mornings did we wake up full of regret and remorse and pledge that we would never again indulge our addiction? And what happened? By noon, or perhaps the next day, week, or month, we had talked ourselves right out of that never-again position and into one of *once-again-and-right-now*. We were as mystified at our relapse as anyone else was. Clearly we knew better, we thought. But we didn't know better. We thought better. On the level of intellect we had seen the futility of using and had given it up. But on the level of the subconscious, where patterns drink their fill, we hadn't seen a thing. A pattern took a break and we labeled it, "Look, I quit drinking, or drugging," or whatever it was that was killing us. We really can't transcend the mind with the mind, but because *mind* keeps telling us that we can, we keep trying.

If we are standing *in* awareness, *as* awareness, then those subtle, directional feelings, a barely noticeable guidance, will come from a higher source, a source beyond ego, and stimulate new, more skillful and compassionate behavior in the world. I don't mean we are somehow being guided by a divine puppet master. What I am saying is that there are always, shall we say, freely floating choices and channels, and the further from the floor we are seeing from, the more likely we are to be guided by higher ones. If we take an honest look, we'll notice that we're nearly always kind to one person—ourselves. From the awakened view, everything and everyone we experience is a version of ourselves. Thus wise behavior for the benefit of all is a natural, effortless outcome.

We first become better receivers, and eventually morph into being better transmitters. We teach what we are, twenty-four hours a day. We transmit it to everyone and everything we come into contact with. Enlightenment is simply seeing from reality instead of a limited position, and the embodiment process is learning to *live* from reality instead of a limited position. How we live is always a louder transmission than what we know. And while there is no *actual* process of development here—you can't improve upon perfection—there certainly is—I believe without exception—a *perceived* process. First we wake up, and then there is a long period of sweeping clouds from corner and sill. Yes, we are always already all-accepting, unmoving, perfectly perfect, primordial awareness. But if *we can't see* it for clouds, then *we can't be it*—not consciously, not knowingly. And of course that seeing-being forever remains an unclaimable space. Trying to own enlightenment is the surest, fastest method of shutting it down.

Here is truth in fraternal twinness, as we spoke about in the beginning of this chapter. We are *in* the dream on one level, and the dream is happening *within us* on another. We are a part *and* we are the whole. We are like holons, by which I mean that we are different, but not truly separate, and within each of us there can be found a full map of the whole. We are both the witness *and* the witnessed; the ocean *and* the drop. We are that which is watching the dream scenes, *and* that which makes up the content of the same scenes. Everything we see is none other than ourselves. The Face of God is everywhere, smiling brilliantly. Mind wants to pick one position or the other and hold to it. Either-or is what it knows, and so that's naturally what it's comfortable with. We, however, are talking about something that is beyond the mind's ability to understand or pigeon-hole.

Let's voyage back to our step.

So, in step four we have begun to spot our unconscious patterns, and got a start at seeing through them in step five. What next? In recovery, we go to a quiet place and make ourselves ready. It's not altogether different in Nonduality. We may or may not be turning to a traditional Higher Power, and we may or may not recognize our patterns as defects, but it is certainly all about raising our willingness factor. Somewhat shockingly, however, it's not just the willingness to be rid of our perceived flaws. It may also include the willingness to *not* be rid of them! There are things we're going to have to live with until we don't. This is acknowledged in recovery, but not a lot of time is spent on it, because there's nothing fixable in it. It's all about true, absolute surrender. This gets very tricky, and it gives ego a sparkling opportunity to co-opt our spirituality, so we really have to approach this step with a great deal of integrity.

We may wonder, since it looks to us that these unconscious patterns don't serve any positive purpose, and since they appear to block us from fully and consciously experiencing our true nature, then why on earth do we have them to begin with? "Why" is a suffering question that also impedes progress. There's a Buddhist story about this kind of thing that I'll borrow.

A monk seeking liberation came to see the Buddha. Many questions were preying on his mind. He asked Buddha about reincarnation and transmigration of the soul, about the nature of infinity and eternity. He went on an on with these metaphysical questions. Buddha told this story. "Suppose a man was shot with a poisoned arrow. The doctor comes to treat him, but before the dying man will accept help, he wants certain information. 'What was the identity and history of my assailant?' he asks. 'Was the arrow shot with long bow, or crossbow? What was my assailant's motivation? What sort of family does he come from?'

Is any of this really important? Time is short! If the man waits for all these questions to be answered before he accepts treatment, then he will die.

Let us be as the Buddha and not as the monk. Let's leave why to the philosophers. Is it not enough to know that *we do* have these unconscious patterns and that they vex us? Are we well served to try to chase down the genesis of our beliefs, opinions, and positions, or is our time not better spent dealing with what already is? We have these patterns. From our limited viewpoint, it appears they do not benefit our lives, or our spiritual quest. In step four we label; in step five we investigate. In the next step we see if we can become willing to either let them go, or let them go on. *Thy will be done*, is our watchword.

The step says, "We were entirely ready to have God remove these defects of character." I interpret that, both in recovery and Nonduality, to mean, "We are entirely surrendered to God's will." The lack of surrender is our real problem—in *everything*. We live in the myth of ourselves and then bitch about "reality." What do we know about reality? If we're viewing things from a mythical me, we know nothing about reality. We know a lot about our stories *about* reality, but nothing of reality itself. Don't believe me; check for yourself.

It's rarely an actual *incident* that we take umbrage to, but rather our *interpretation* of the incident. Unless it's instinctual behavior, such as dodging a striking snake, or a speeding car, we are always reacting to our own thinking, never the facts on the ground. When coming from instinct, we simply jump to the side of snakes and cars, which is fine. We could say that we find ourselves *having jumped* to the side. Biology takes care of itself. The organism is built to survive. In between the spotting of the danger and the end of the reaction to it, there was no self, no me present to interfere. This is an example of *wu wei*, or actionless action. There is a quite plausible theory that *wu wei* doesn't incur karmic bonds, but who really knows? None of us are dead, and thus we can't be sure. What matters for us is simply *noticing* the action, not slicing and dicing it afterward. This is just what the Buddha told his monk.

When the mind steps in, it generally makes a mess, because it superimposes layers of story onto every situation. The snake becomes an evil snake, or a vengeful snake, or a punishing snake. It goes from something to simply be avoided to something terrifying, something that's trying to kill us, that may kill us, that almost *did* kill us! It shouldn't be there, it shouldn't do that, and on, and on. The car is being driven by someone careless, reckless, stupid, drunk, old, foreign, whatever. They should know better, they should do better! Where are the police when you need them? And on, and on.

In the absence of truth, there is always story. In the absence of story, there is always truth.

We were just speaking of death in our Buddha story, so let's take a moment and look at it, simply because it's such a looming question for us. Many of us get into seeking because we are "scared to death of death." As a matter of fact, most of us are so busy dreading our deaths, and wondering "what happens to me afterward," that we miss out on living our lives *prior* to the "afterward"! We sleep our lives away and then we die. We could call total surrender a sort of death, and it is one that opens up the possibility for us to live freely and fully now. This is what's important about life—living. I'm confident death will take care of itself; let's leave it to the experts—the dead. Here we are keen on becoming experts at living!

I will tell you that I am extremely comfortable with my own theories of death and that whole ball of wax. I'm comfortable with my theories about the Big Bang, the end of the world, and any number of other "imponderables," as the Buddha called them. Perhaps we'll talk about them someday. But not here! We are going to take the Buddha's good and practical advice, and work with our experience of here and now. As we do that more and more for longer and longer we may notice that these really crushing questions naturally fall to the side. Most of them are made moot rather than answered, because most of these questions stem from the ego. When the ego is seen through, so are its questions.

I remember the first time I ever quit drinking in a serious way. It didn't last long. I was so concerned about what I was going to do on vacation. If I couldn't drink on vacation, what was the point? What I couldn't see, or wouldn't see, was that I didn't have a *job*. I couldn't keep one for my drinking. I had never stayed at a company long enough to even *get* a vacation. I took vacations *between* jobs—most people called it unemployment. This is just how we get caught up in chasing down hypothetical answers to hypothetical questions instead of brushing our teeth and combing our hair with full attention.

Thus this concludes our short discussion about death and other imponderables! It's just this sort of birdie that we look at all our lives, never noticing the photographer with a hundred pounds of gear right in front of us.

Understanding and surrender are synonyms. If we understand the nature of reality, we surrender to *what is*. If we surrender to *what is*, we discover the nature of reality. What ego is an absolute *genius* at doing is taking an impersonal universe and making every aspect of it personal. Let us understand that an impersonal universe does not mean a cold one. That again is ego's take on a word it doesn't like. An *impersonal* universe doesn't mean an *anti-personal* universe. If we look closely, we'll notice that an anti-personal universe would just be the flip side of a personal one; it's a 180, and it's indicative that our thinking is still all about us. Let's look at an example.

Let's say we're driving along and we pull a thoughtless maneuver in traffic. We were in our head, caught up in a pattern of thinking and being, and while being *caught up* in our make-believe world, we were *removed from* the real world and its happenings. Thus we went against, or varied from, the natural flow around us, and it hasn't gone unnoticed. Someone has popped us with a raised finger, or fist, fried us with "the look," or cursed us out loud for our carelessness. Without our personalizing the event, what's actually going on? I don't mean in metaphysical terms, I mean in practical terms. What does our *body* report?

A horn is sounding. A person is motioning with their hand. A frightened, frustrated look is thrown. Someone is making noise. That's what the body tells us. That's all there is to it until we decide to own it, to make it about an imaginary me. There is no situation so bad that ego cannot step in and make it worse. That's its job: starting fires and fueling them. What is it that's below the anger that fires up when someone attacks us, or our actions? It's the same thing that's below the anger that ignites when someone (in our opinion) drives too slowly, brakes too fast, changes lanes irresponsibly, runs a light, or makes some other similar offense. Either condition is a direct, personal threat to us, and our sovereignty over our personal world. What is it that lives in such an ever-perilous position? Ego. There are no other candidates.

The other person is actually grading our *activity*, our *verbness*. We, however, have accepted it as a threat and an insult to our *personal* person, the very *entityness* of us. Let's notice that our verbness is true: it's out there in the world for anyone to see. If there's a security camera watching the street, they can play it back and show the scene to us—both our verbness and our "assailant's" verbness. But that same camera cannot show us any trace of entityness. There's no trace, because there's no entity other than in our heads. The camera will show *driving*—an activity that is a combined motion brought forward when a vehicle is paired with an animal behind its wheel. If it's a human animal, then driving may be more or less skillful—or not! In this instance, in one frame the vehicles would be seen to be a safe distance apart. In the next they'd be dangerously close, and in the third, they are again a safe distance apart. That's the real movie. There's not much to it. Simple.

If it's a really good camera with a sharp lens, then it may catch a motioning hand. If it has audio, it will record some shrieking sounds.

But it will not be able to catch the pair of storms that are now roaring in both animals' heads. That's because these are, indeed, *human* animals, and unlike dogs, cats, and lizards, they are not living in the *actual* movie, meaning the movie the camera can catch and replay. These human animals are living in the story they're *making up* to flesh out, enhance and, most importantly, personalize the bare events occurring. If they were living in actual events, they'd just drive on. The past is over. Any potential threat has passed. Unless the players involved in this scene create the story of continuing threat via the magic of personalization.

Personalization solidifies the make-believe "me" for each of our drivers. In the absence of resistance, which stems wholly from the act of personalization, there is just what the camera catches. Life moves on, the way gazelles do in the wild after being threatened by a predator. They dodge, they regroup, they eat, sleep, or mate. The past is immediately *over*. They don't stand around telling each other stories about what "might have been," or what "should have been." The gazelle's brains register the facts perfectly. The only thing that happened was what actually happened. There is no *what isn't*. There is only *what is*, and *what is*, at this regrouped moment, is to be found in the shapes and flavors of the lush grass in front of them.

Our point here is not to learn how to drive better, which might be a terrific side benefit, but rather to learn to see and tell the truth. Or, we might say, to simply learn to see and then not lie about it. It's unnecessary for me to embroider *what is* with *what isn't*. Reality happens to be quite full and satisfying all by itself. Like Goldilocks' bed and porridge, it is neither too large or too warm, nor too small or too cold. Reality is always just right. It won't sustain *identities*, mind you, but every moment is full and satisfying without them.

Our drivers' stories, however, may never end. People maintain random resentments for decades. As they say in the rooms, this is like taking poison and expecting the other person to die. The two drivers' stories will be wildly different even though they are in reaction to the same event. That's because stories stem from a point of view, and these two points of view are quite divergent. Or are they? They are actually *symbiotic*. Both animals get just what they need from the clash, which is mutual support for their personal stories of me-ness and other-ness; of victimship and self-pity. Everyone may be upset, but better to be upset than nonexistent!

If we look closely we can easily see that this is the primary tradeoff in life, our most fundamental agreement. Fear and anger are the antidotes to nonexistence. If I'm worried then I'm "here," on planet, and holding up as a separate entity. The very same thing happens with anger, because anger and fear are the flip sides of each other, the two make-believe 180s. They cloud the view of the the real 360, that this incident was simply an appearance within wholeness. It's a manifestation of the one thing going on, and causes no suffering in and of itself.

We will only *own* the insult (anger) or threat (fear) that a fist or a finger, or look, or curse represents if we think there's something to it. Has this guy found us out at last? He's saying we're stupid. He's saying we're careless. He's saying we're selfish to the point of reck-lessness. And we, of course, fear that he may be right, which makes us scared and angry! So, in order to puff up the "me" balloon that is constantly sagging under its own weight, we step right in and help the other driver do his job by translating his action as personal, just as he did ours. We don't normally take our life advice from hot-headed maniacs, but for this guy we're making an exception! We're taking what he says to heart, and breathing a sigh of relief at the same time. "We," the separate "me", remain alive for another few minutes, the few minutes it takes for us to find a fresh threat or complaint. Large threats and complaints have a bit of lasting power, most come and go within minutes, or even seconds. Complaining is just a strategy for keeping ego alive, for propping up our false story of independent existence. There's just one thing going on.

We know just how everything should be. We have the perfect, though ever-evolving, blueprint of just how things should be at every moment, including the imaginary moments of past and future. And if you look closely and honestly, it's never like... *this*. We live in an ongoing *argument* in our heads in order to take our stand as independent entities instead of awareness.

With the dream of separation comes the dream of threat. They are hand in glove, only they cannot be pulled apart. One cannot exist without the other. When we take on identification with the idea of "being," then we automatically have to also face the horror of "not being." We can disappear just as easily as we appeared. Poof! It only takes a second either way. Deep down we know the absolute truth about ourselves; we know our absolute nature. By default, that means we also know the truth about our false selves, these billions of precariously balanced "little me's." We appear to discover something new upon awakening, but what we really discover is what we knew all along. *There is only one thing going on and we are it.* To invite the "visitation" of truth is to invite the death of the individual me. This is the most frightening concept of all. Yet in that so-called death is the recovery of our absolute nature, a whole other level of recovery. We die, but we do not die in vain.

Understandably, there are not a lot of takers for this dying thing. However, let's be clear that nothing can die that does not first live. The separate me is a dream to begin with; it does not actually exist. All that dies is the belief in the separate me; not the personality, and certainly not the *sense of being* that we truly are, but which we have erroneously, and foolishly, assigned as being the property of a single, solitary human being, the speck within a speck in the outback of a backwoods galaxy. We have to be willing to let the insanity of me-ness die.

In a sense, we have all already died to get where we are now, to be clean, sober, free of the terrible confusion that is addiction. We had to be willing to let our addict die. We had to see the truth of our lives, and let the lies die: the entitlement, the arrogance, the insularity, and the resentments. As addicts, we know a lot about dying. Was it worth it to let the old life die so that we could embrace the new one we found in recovery? It was for me, I know that much.

I'm now suggesting—no—I am *declaring* that there is yet more available—an indescribable peace, the peace that surpasses understanding, lies just on the other side of this death. And don't worry, the ego doesn't really die. It can't, because it's just thoughts, it's not really a thing, and thus not capable of dying. Let's say that we *apparently* have an ego. I call my apparent ego Lazarus, because it won't die for more than three days at a time! There's still plenty of ego here, I just don't pay it much attention, and I don't advise anyone to either! That's not much of a problem; I am ignored by droves!

Remember back when we were faced with giving up our addictions in the *present moment*? In all likelihood we had talked about the benefits of sanity and abstinence for years. We'd quit, sure we would. It was always easy to quit in the *future*. That *do-it-now* thing, however, when cravings were ripping through our bodies, that was a totally different thing. This was not easy, this was not fun, this was not the way it was supposed to be. But for one reason or another, through guts or grace or sheer luck, we did not answer craving's call. And what happened? In my case everything got worse! That's always the case, is it not? And then, slowly, it got better. And better. And better! It's so good now that I'm embarrassed to report on it, so I won't. Suffice it to say that I am *happy*!

Without the paramount belief in this separate me, life takes on a new lightness, a new innocence, and a new excitement over the ordinary. Uncertainty and unknowing are experienced joyfully! The more the experience becomes grounded, the lighter the world shows up for us. We may not get what the personality wants, but we notice that the personality adapts to wanting what it gets. Everything is new—over and over again! Everything fits, and everything is seen to be amazing. We can be dazzled by cheese toast or an apple. We can be knocked off our feet by a rainstorm—or a single drop of dew hanging on the edge of a flower petal. Within the shampoo we've just poured into our palm we see the universe, radiant and pulsing. Within the universe we see just one thing going on. And it is *perfect*.

The degree to which we embrace wholeness will be the measure of our peace, our security, and our serenity. Usually we find out who and what we are by way of who and what we are not. If we are beginning to sense our *onionness*, that we are layer upon layer of something built upon a core of nothing, then we are as ready as we are ever going to be to move on to the next step.

CHAPTER SEVEN
Step Seven

WILLINGNESS

THIS STEP IS VERY SIMPLE, AND WE'RE NOT GOING TO COMPLICATE IT here. It is covered in a single paragraph within the granddaddy of all recovery, and all recovery literature, the Big Book of Alcoholics Anonymous. In that tradition, it is a clean and easy petitionary prayer, asking God to take away what *we* have designated as being our shortcomings. The prayer specifically says, "I pray that you now remove from me every single defect of character which stands in the way of my usefulness to you and my fellows." The wonderful thing is that it does not then go on to *list* what it is that should be removed, and what should be left alone.

If we focus *on the words of this prayer*, then I don't see very much difference between how it would be taken in traditional recovery, or how it would be seen Nondually. If we're really serious, then we're in, or we're out. Either way, we're once again fully relinquishing our will and our life—our "bondage of self," that the third step prayer talks about—to our Higher Power. This is just another way to put across the same idea. Again like the third step prayer, we are saying, "Do with me as *thou* wilt." We are giving over our make-believe sovereignty in favor of the real sovereignty of *what is*. Reality rules, and here we are acknowledging that. Well, either we are, or we're going to be frustrated as hell. I'll go with acknowledgment.

What are we supposed to be like? Just like we are until we're different. How do we know this? Because there's not so much as a shred of evidence pointing in any other direction. We may wish to be different; we may dearly long to be different. Others may desire it for us. But we're not, at least until we are.

We simply can't know what needs to take place in our character's make-up; what should be dropped and what should be kept. How could we? We can only pretend to know such things if we're first pretending to be a separate me from a world of "other." From some angle I'm sure the Grand Canyon looks like a damn big hole that someone should get busy and fill up. It's a geologic *error* that someone needs to fix! Our human viewpoint on all things is infinitesimal and the universe is vast beyond imagining. If we tell ourselves the truth, then we have to confess that we are lost, absolutely clueless beyond the clues in front of our faces, which is a wonderful place for us to be. Without a judging center, otherwise known as a "me," we can have no idea of how things should be, beyond what they already are. That includes how *we are*, too! We don't even know what *job* our body is to do, other than what it's currently doing. We don't have to wait for things to be right! They're *already* right! Always. Any opinion that differs from reality is a doorway to unlimited suffering at the hands of mind.

We may notice that we're only troublemakers when we think that we are "found," meaning we think we know what's going on, and have developed an agenda which we're convinced is "best for everyone," which is simply *code* for "best for me." In the end, however, we cause the most trouble for ourselves. We can't move beyond what we think we know until we can see clearly that we don't know anything at all, not in the deepest sense.

What appear to be our most tragic failings often make us more valuable tools. Without the story of our failure, we have no way to relate to other addicts. Had we not seen firsthand that we have a striking inability to satisfactorily manipulate our world, we probably would not have found ourselves becoming interested in Nonduality. Given this odd truism, we live most freely when we're open to having what we see as our shortcomings left in place—even at our own apparent expense. If we took the third step with genuine sincerity, then our life is no longer "all about us." Of course it was *never* about us, because there *is* no "us," but for the moment we are speaking conventionally.

Now, let's be clear that not all of us are praying folk. Nonduality encompasses everything, not just the parts of the world we agree with. So, everyone gets to do what they do. They're doing it anyway, but now we're not suffering. Thus others pray or they don't—who cares? All that matters to us is what *we* do.

Certainly some of us have a quite undefined notion of a Higher Power. I fall into that camp myself. I can *witness* reality, I can *be* reality, but I certainly can't define it. But I surely wouldn't let any of this stop me from praying. I'm keenly aware of all the paradoxes. Again, who cares? Beyond our haughty intellectual prejudices, what do we actually *know* about such things? Very little, I'll wager. I've come to know much less since I woke up, not much more. Let's forget for a moment both the concepts of separation *and* of nonseparation. Look at them: they're 180's! Reality, the full 360, is beyond both. From a holographic standpoint praying sort of makes sense. The apparent drop prays to the apparent ocean in a reality where neither one really exists! We don't have to go down this road very far; it's dizzying. I'm doing so only for the sake of knocking some of the sureness out of us.

By the same token, I'm certainly not trying to convince anyone to pray. I just don't want anyone thinking they should *not* pray. If you notice yourself praying it's fine. If you notice that you don't, that's also fine. I encourage you not to pray—if you don't. So I encourage you to pray—if you do. My point here is that we simply shouldn't limit ourselves, and we especially shouldn't limit ourselves while sitting upon lofty, theoretically absolute, intellectual perches. Did you ever notice that the higher we climb the further we fall, and the more it hurts when we land on our butts?

We want to stay open to the whole field of possibilities. When we notice sureness slipping in, let us quickly inquire into it until we find the place of not knowing. That place will always be there if we're willing to look. In fact, it's the only thing that's ever really there. All conventional knowing is manufactured; it's not inherent. If you want to pray, have at it. My wife and I still say grace over every meal we have at home. We just *like* it. It's homey, it's celebratory, and it helps us to keep us from taking good food and good company for granted. We don't do so when we go out, because we see it as too much of a show.

In general, however, Nonduality could be called the philosophy of not asking the universe to do anything it's not already doing. In this tradition we're not applying for change. We're applying only for awareness and acceptance. Both of those are already here, so what we're *really* after is simply recognition. If change is resultant from clearer seeing, fine. If it's not, fine. Here, we know that we don't know what's best. This is no small matter; it's a big deal to know that you don't know what's best. When sureness is removed from someone, it'll take out most of their poison along with it. Our primary job on this path is to lose the certainty of what we think we know, and then to not build a new identity around what's left—not even around the idea that we are now superior "don't-knowers"!

Certainty is the worst disease we can catch if we're on the Nondual path. None of us may have much effect on *the* world, but all of us have a hell of a large effect on *our* world. Our world is entirely our projection. There is no such thing as an objective fact, or an objective truth. They are all projections of underlying BOPs—beliefs, opinions, and positions—at the crossroads of a given situation. Conditioning meets circumstance. When we float in no-place-to-stand, our world is a constantly unfolding mystery. Like origami, we see one surface at a time. Like spies, it's all on a need-to-know basis. When we are sure, however, then we are stuck with having to manage things, and we talked about the futility of that in the first step.

Is sureness really a certain path to suffering? How could it be otherwise? Forget what anyone else knows. Let's examine what *we* know. We only decide we know how things should be when we notice that *what is* isn't suiting us. That immediately puts us in opposition with reality. We only decide we know how people should behave when we see that they aren't already doing so. Knowing bred from sureness is always contrary to what's happening.

When we live in not knowing, where is there any opposition to *what is*? Resistance is ego's "selfness"; it is its body and blood; it is its borders and limits. Without resistance there is only a freely flowing world, always changing, always transmuting, washing this thing in, and that thing out, and then reversing the tide. The world of form is circular, and never-ending. Nothing in the show is static, but the show itself is never ending. In fact, there is nothing *but* show.

Even if my Higher Power, by my judgment, has got some of the show wrong, how likely is it that he or she needs me to pick out and point out which parts those are? I am a wrecker of lives and worlds, not a builder. Left to my own devices—a state I worked tirelessly to bring about—I wound up living in a park as a drunken bum, a broken human in an extraordinarily dark corner of the dream. I threw away or ruined every good thing that came into my life for thirty-five years. I wound up in recovery begging for someone to save my unhelpful, unjust, unsavory life. And now *I* think *I* know what's right for the *world*?

Oh please. It makes me laugh.

I ask again, what do we really know? What do we really know that we are sure is true? How can we be judge and jury, much less executioner, ourselves or anyone else? Yet we regularly fill all three positions, do we not? Do we really have such great wisdom, do we see with a God's-eye view? It's a hypothetical question, because surely we do not. None of us do; none of us can. We are lost, but we don't *want* to be lost, because we wrongly think it's frightening instead of freeing. So we invent stories of being grounded, sure, and secure, and then we build our lives around those stories. We can and will defend them—especially with *someone else's* life! Communal stories make up the myths that countries are bound by, and war is never more than a step away from a challenged collective belief system. A sure person is a danger to themselves and others; a sure country is a danger to the planet. A sure planet cannot long stand.

I know the one thing I really know. And I know it to be true. *I Am.* I know that I Am, because I cannot *not* be. To say that I am not, there has to be something here saying that. The contrary statement ends up making the initial point. *What* I am, I don't know. I don't have a clue. *Why* I am? It's a moot point: I am. *Where* am I? Here, outside of space. *When* am I? Now, outside of time. I Am.

I am this—*this* very this! Here! Now! When I reach out my hand and touch the spaciousness that appears to be surrounding me, I am touching my very own body *with* my very own body, *within* my own body. Everything here has *already* been accepted. It cannot exist and fail to have already been accepted—by *me!* Everything here is *already* embraced in boundless, all-accepting love. I am automatically healed when I see that I am whole. I am unbroken, unbound, unfettered, and unafraid!

There is just one thing going on, and it is always already *perfect.* When I hold this in my heart I find it full of joy. When I hold it up for examination I find it wonderfully empty. Existence neither explains nor justifies. It *is,* and that is *enough.* Even as the body dies it feels the strong hands of existence wrapping themselves around it, lifting it, cradling it in its warm arms until all trace of individuality disappears. I am beyond resistance. I am beyond suffering. Those are stories, too.

I Am.

In the end, this "I Am" is all that is left. It's all that's here right now. It's all that ever was. In the beginning was the Word. The Proverbs say, "I was appointed from eternity, from the beginning, from before the world began." And I will be here when it ends. Amen.

I Am.

There is only one thing going on, and it is perfect. As our story begins to change, to apparently evolve, let us willingly, vigorously carry to the light all the many aggregates that make us up, the sheer flotsam and jetsam that have been thrown together, which have temporarily compounded, and to which we have erroneously given name. Let the unshaded light itself decide what is to remain dark, and let it replace what is to disappear *with* the light of knowing awareness, *through* the light of knowing awareness, *for* the light of knowing awareness.

We will be attempting to do just this in the next two steps.

CHAPTER EIGHT
Step Eight

ACCEPTANCE

IN THE RECOVERY TRADITION, THE ACCEPTANCE WE'RE TALKING about in this step is full acceptance of *responsibility* for our past; full enough that we're willing to make things right even at a high personal cost. As someone who went to jail over what he put on this list, you can imagine that I did and do consider this a vitally important move towards living "clean and serene," as they say, whether we're in recovery or out. You don't have to be an addict to benefit from the steps we have taken, but few will take them who are not in the deepest sort of pain. Like recycling wrecks from a junkyard into new cars, from crushing defeat fresh beings are built.

From a Nondual perspective, there's no list needed for our work here, because there's just one thing going on, and therefore, at least from the absolute view, there is just one amends that ever needs to be made. If we had a list at all, it would consist of a single line and say simply, "the nameless." It's not that we've hurt the one thing going on; it can't be hurt. Nor have we offended it; it can't be offended. There's nothing whatsoever that we can do *to* or *for* the nameless one thing going on, because it is everything, and it is us. So how about this amends thing? Are we to ignore it? I don't think so.

This amend is *truly* a mending. We want to give our energy and attention to closing the imaginary gap between self and Self. Just because there is no *real* gap, does not negate our addressing the *appearance* of one. In a mind-wrenching way, so long as it *feels like* there's a gap, there's a gap! Our confusion—which results in personal, psychological suffering—arises out of this misunderstanding, and no sweeping intellectual gesture is going to quiet that.

The most fundamental causes of our sense of separation are our beliefs, opinions and positions, our BOPs. Key among these is our sense, our feeling, that our Higher Power is somewhere else, somewhen else: we invent a story of space and time, and then *we place* divinity somewhere in an imaginary forgotten corner, in an imaginary future time. Once we puncture this illusion, then we discover that our body is not just a grain of sand on the beach, but rather that it is the whole beach, the ocean, the planet—indeed, the entire universe. In the absence of a story about boundaries there *are no* boundaries.

Let's share a quick but very profound experience, and then a story which may highlight our quandary. Wherever you are, please read this exercise and then close your eyes and do what the exercise asks. As simple as this one is, reading about an exercise is just not enough, so please participate. Participatory spirituality is effective spirituality.

Excercise 6: The Body of God

✳

Put your hand out at arm's length and run it through the air. Move it back and forth, up and down, and draw big circles. Now open your eyes. What I'm going to tell you is not the truth, but it's very close to the truth—*close enough*, at this stage. Like the finger of doubting Thomas, you have just run your arm and hand through the body of God. It's right there, right *here*, surrounding you, me, all of us, everything, everywhere, all the time. It is not *other than* you, me, all of us, everything, everywhere, all the time. Space, or rather spaciousness, we could say, is the "body" of God.

I know, it's just too simple. It's too easy. It could never in a million years be that simple and easy—unless it is. You don't have to believe me. Test it out yourself with some hard questions and see if they don't at least point in that direction. Nonduality is always about your own evidence, gathered and experienced firsthand. So ask away. Where does that space begin? Where does it end? When was it born? When do you think it will die? Do these questions even make sense when applied to spaciousness?

What *time* is it in pure, empty space? I'm not asking about a world that might be contained within space, but rather about the space itself. Does time even apply? How can it? No, time does not apply to empty space. What *volume* does space take up? Things take up volume in space, but does spaciousness itself have volume? Of course not. In order to have a physical world, we must have volume and duration. Nothing can be seen without that pair operating together. Again, don't trust my word; examine it yourself. Can a moon exist without volume? No, there has to be *something within* the clear void of space if we're to see it, and that something within cannot exist in the absence of volume. Even then, we're only half-way there. That moon must exist within volume for a *period of time* in order for us to see it. Volume cannot exist without time. No time, no volume, no perception. No perception, no moon. We might have a conceptual moon in our heads without physical perception, but we're talking about the real world, the world where our body is living, not the imaginary world in our heads. We're going by our own direct experience here, not imagination, books or other hearsay.

Space simply *is*. It's the one unchanging, eternal, infinite "nothing" that exists. We can't even say it's "one"; that's saying too much. One implies a second and spaciousness is beyond that. That's why some traditions say there is only "not-two." Space *is*. That's really all that can be said about it. Have you noticed how similar space is to the sense of being we worked with in chapter two? Uncanny, is it not?

Is this "description" of space, which can only be described *via negativa*—by what it's not—is this not, just as the sense of being

CHAPTER 8 — ACCEPTANCE   117

was earlier, beginning to sound like descriptions we've heard applied to *divinity*? Is it not possible that the marvelous mystery is existing with us, upon us, inside of us, indeed, *as us*, precisely here and now, and nowhere or nowhen else?

✳

Let's look even a little further. What are other words the heralded mystics of all traditions, East and West, have used for thousands of years when trying to convey the nature of the truth of our being? "Stillness" is pretty common, is it not? Where might we find stillness if we were to look for it? Might it not be even closer than "right under our noses"? This stillness, otherwise known as space, is what our noses actually appear within!

Notice that everything that arises in the world is actually a movement, large and slow, or small and fast, or some other combination, but a movement nonetheless. A mountain arises out of the earth, lasts seemingly forever in human terms, but eventually, like everything else, they wear away. We tend to think about time in human terms, but our lives are essentially immeasurable blips if we switch our view to geologic time. In geologic time, mountains come, and mountains go. Continents smash together and break apart. The seas and continents ice up, then melt, then ice up again. From a mountain's view, we would appear to be born, live and die as fast as the bloom of a queen of the night cactus does to us: from promise, to full form, to fade out, all within a few hours. And geologic time, already essentially unfathomable to us, *withers* compared to astronomical time. Planets like the earth rise and fall; their solar systems do the same—even galaxies come and go within astronomical time!

What is the movement, or rather the lack of movement, that all of these arise from and fall back into? They arise and fall within space, which we could say is simply stillness; stillness is the very definition of space. It does not move. Without the "background" of this all-containing, ever-present, never-moving stillness, movement could not even be noticed. As a metaphorical truth, we could say space is the screen upon which the movie of the world is played. Although there is no volume or duration within stillness, without that stillness' *capacity* for volume and duration, there is only void.

"Silence" is another way mystics of all times have described the ground of being. What is this silence of which they speak? Where can we find it? Is it not right here? Is it not another word for this same spaciousness—this same, limitless *capacity*? Every sound, from a baby's cry to a drum solo, has two common characteristics. They arise from silence, and they fall back into silence. First there was silence, then there was sound. At the end of the sound, silence is still there. Silence has not arisen; sound has simply fallen away. Silence never moved. It is always there, before and after, and in between as well, though we lose our knowledge of it while sound is happening. Silence is the "screen" within which sound *happens*, just as space is the screen within which form *moves*. The play of sound can be also be seen as the movement of form, for sound is indeed a type of form. Of what is sound composed? It is composed of waves, is it not? And the waves expand ever-outward seemingly against, yet actually within—stillness.

Let's now discuss the three historical attributes of divinity before we leave this and go into a story. The "possibilities" we'll look at next have already been proven factual to me to my *complete* satisfaction. What's fact to me, however, at this point may still be theory to you. So, I'm not asking you to believe any of this. I have already had these points answered to my satisfaction. In the spirit of scientific investigation, I now present them for peer review. You look at it for yourself.

A. OMNIPRESENCE

This is the easiest of the three points to agree on. Science backs up our common sense and intuition. Space is everywhere. It is what holds everything, and it is, at the very least, within everything. From galaxies to electrons, our universe is all about space. It is singularly everywhere; it has no competition. I will not insult either one of us by bothering to further "prove" anything so obvious.

B. OMNISCIENCE

We have, presumably, already agreed that space is omnipresent, an attribute that is typically applied to, and reserved for, divinity. So the first *new* thing I'm going to declare is that this omnipresent no-thing is omniscient as well. Granted I can't prove with a calculator or a chalkboard that this is a fact, but if an honest investigator looks closely at its key attribute of omnipresence, then space, *better than anything else,* has the *potential* to be omniscient. After all, in the absence of time or volume, every imaginary point in space is hooked up to ever other imaginary point without the slightest resistance or interference. There is no time or distance factor to be overcome, and so wherever there is anything to be known, then space, if it was unfathomably intelligent and overflowing with aliveness, *could* know everything everywhere all at the same time.

In the end, all that would be required would be for the one thing going on to know *itself.* I'm simply saying it does. The unfathomable intelligence and overflowing aliveness are available to be experienced firsthand, by every reader. Many of you doubtlessly *will* experience it. Many others will intuit it. The attribute of omniscience then becomes as self-evident as omnipresence.

C. OMNIPOTENCE

We cannot deny that space is omnipresent. I don't see a reasonable argument against the *potential* for omniscience, and unless all the mystics of every age, including *this* one, are a bunch of brazen liars, or practical jokers, then I think it fair to say there is quite a lot of evidence pointing to the fact that it is, in fact, omniscient. An interesting question to ask here might be, "How many 'spaces' are there?" I count *one*. This count also matches up with my own experience of there being only one thing going on. If we can accept for the moment that this is true, where would you guess the juice is coming from that is feeding the births of both galaxies and guppies? How is it that electrons orbit, birds chirp, waves move, winds blow, and stars collapse? All of the juice for everything has to be coming from something. Where could that source be?

That's an easy one, is it not? If there's only one thing going on, then that power has to come from... the one thing going on. We have already said that space is everywhere; that point was a no-brainer. We cannot prove that anything else exists *everywhere*. The evidence is heavy that space *is* the one thing going on. If that is so, then it is clearly omnipotent.

I'm not suggesting this little exercise does or should satisfy your questions. I am suggesting that you go ahead and wake up, at which point all of these questions will be answered to *your* complete satisfaction just as they have been here. Let's go now to a story that may help us see why many people are where they are, namely, *stuck*. Divinity doesn't need to be found; it cannot be *avoided*! If we're looking for liberation, then it only needs to be recognized. This isn't rocket science. Any fool can see it. Only a knower cannot.

Excercise 7: The Living Room

*

Let's pretend that we are both sitting in my living room, and you're my revered spiritual teacher. We've been together for a while now, and although I've clawed around the edges, and beaten on the roof, I've just never quite been able to walk through the Gateless Gate. I've never been able to "get it," as they say. On this day you've just taken me through the wave-your-hand exercise contained in the early part of this chapter. You explain to me, as slowly and clearly as you can, that I have just run my hand through the body of God. "In fact," you tell me, "we could say that the *hand* of God has just been run through the *body* of God by the *power* of God. That's because there's just one thing going on, Fred, and *we are it*! We are entirely *enclosed* by divinity; we are entirely *composed* of divinity. We have met the great mystery, and it is *us!*"

Suddenly, less from the information than from the timing, I feel like I've been hit with a hammer right in the middle of my forehead. I am stunned, completely taken aback; thrown into total awe and wonderment! I can hardly catch my breath. "So God is right *here*? Right here in my *living room*? Is that what you're saying?"

"That's *exactly* what I'm saying," you tell me, smiling. You can see it on my face. You can see it in the growing smile. Here, at last, is marked progress from even the *poorest* of students! At long last, Fred is GETTING IT!

My head is whirling. Tears begin to well. I cry out, " You mean RIGHT NOW? God is in my living room right now? This is *it*?"

You nod your head and smile beatifically. This is great! "Yes, Fred," you say with the greatest satisfaction imaginable. "That's why you could never find it, and why you never would. You can't *find* what's *already here*. You've been searching for something objective, and there's *nothing objective* to find. You have, in some way, been looking for a noun. God is not a noun, it's a *verb*, and it's right here in your living room; right here *with us, as us* at this very moment. Call it 'space' or 'spaciousness' for the sake of convenience. That's an easy way to kind of 'see' the unseeable. It's not quite a true description, because there isn't a *true* description, but it's about as close as we can get. Whatever it is, it is alive! Whatever it is, it is intelligent beyond imagining. And of course, as you see now, it is the one thing going on."

I'm still shaking my head in amazement, and we're both starting to laugh. "Unbelievable!" I say. "It's so *simple*! I've been making this thing so complex for all these years, and it's been *right here, right now*, presenting itself for all to see, for every moment that ever was. THIS IS *IT*!"

"That's right," you tell me. "That's why we overlook it, because it's so direct; it's so here and now. In the end, it's self-evident, is it not? There's absolutely no-thing to get!" You beam joyfully.

"I'm *so* happy," I tell you. "I just have one more question."

"Okay," you say. "What's that?"

"Can you tell me *how* I can get to my living room?"

"WHAT?" you scream.

"How can I get to my living room so that I can come to union with the ground of my own being?"

You can't believe what you're hearing. So close! Maybe you can yet snatch victory from the jaws of defeat. "Fred! This is *madness*! Look at what the hell you're saying! I've just told you, *it's* already here; *you're* already here. This is IT! You could see that just a bare *moment* ago!"

"How about if I gave up meat?"

"What in God's name are you talking about now?"

"I'm thinking that if I gave up meat, and somehow purified my body, then maybe I could get to my living room, and meet my Higher Power face to face. Or maybe colonics would do it. What do you think is the best *method*?"

"Fred, you've *already met* your Higher Power face to face! It's right here! Right with us! It always was, and always will be! Remember waving your hand around in 'the body of God'? Do that again, for crying out loud. You're no better than Peter in the Garden of Gethsemane. You are denying divinity to save your ego's skin!"

I am unmoved, and am now just being patient with my dear, but foolish old teacher. "Do you think meditation would help me find my living room? Do you think twice a day would do it? Do I need to go on retreat? I bet a retreat would do it."

"Fred, Fred, Fred. Practices are not going to help you find God. We just saw that. Not now. They can't help you find what's already found. You just have to give up this insanity. You have to quit denying the truth if you're ever going to find it. You have to want clarity more than you want your story."

I am still counting off my possibilities. "The Sufis dance. Should I dance? Or drum? The Tibetans drum, and a lot of aborigine religions do too. I think I might like drumming. How about chanting; that's really popular. *Come on*, you're supposed to be my teacher! What good are you if you can't help me get to my living room?"

"You are *in* your goddamn living room right this very second!"

"Well, if you can't help, I think I'll try going to India. A lot of people go there in search of God. I'm not sure how many find her, but it's a bang-up tourist industry, I know that. I bet there's an exotic guru somewhere in the world who can give me clear directions on how to get to my living room. I don't think it would cost me more than five or ten grand to go to India for a while. I could sell my car. That's it. I'll sell my car."

"That's right," you say, in a weary, hoarse, totally exasperated voice. "Go to India, you poor, seeking bastard. That's why the bear went over the mountain, the chicken crossed the road, and Fred went to India. Because they *couldn't not* do it. Go ahead and leave *right now*, why don't you? Come to think of it, since we're in your living room, *I* can actually leave! And I will. *Goodbye.*"

"Goodbye!" you say with a smile. "And thanks for all the great information. I'm really getting it now, and I'm sure I'll see it all better *tomorrow.*"

*

I know this story sounds ridiculous, and it is ridiculous. Nonetheless, this is one of the most commonplace, if unspoken exchanges between teachers and students in Nonduality. It happens in nearly every meeting. It happens when virtually every clear spiritual book is read. It happens with almost every CD, DVD, or MP3 where Nonduality is the teaching point. It happens thousands of times a month on my website, and every website similar to it. The truth is there, in all of those places. It's not hidden at all; it's blasted out from the four corners of the globe every day. It's totally unavoidable. Perhaps not every Nondual teacher is a good one, but from what I've heard, and read, and seen, the great, vast majority of them *have* seen the truth; they know who they are; they have at least *experienced* an awakening, regardless of whether or not they are enlightened in any given moment, to any given arising.

This mock conversation we've just witnessed is what denial looks like when it's put down in black and white. It may not be *intentional* denial, but it's denial nonetheless. The easiest way to begin to overcome this apparent split, at the point where we've begun to understand this thing intellectually, but just can't quite feel it deeply in our gut, is to step on up and take our stand as the one thing going on. We simply *acknowledge* what we already are, and begin to view and act in the world as that reality.

Awakening can be explosive, but just as often it's quiet. I advise you not to look for a specific state beforehand, and I *certainly* advise you not to look for one later. Spiritual experiences come and go. Enlightenment is forever, because in the end there is nothing *but* enlightenment. And there's no end to this thing; I'd go ahead and give up on that notion if I were you. It unfolds, and unfolds, and unfolds.

Oddly enough, when we change our view of the world, the world will begin to respond. Our world will always unquestioningly cooperate with us. It will begin to confirm our viewpoint—whichever one we take—right away, and it will build up steam as it goes. The longer we hold to a point of view, the more *our* world reshapes itself to conform to it. *Our* world is the only world we can know anything about. We can't quite get our minds around this whole thing, and we don't need to. Like recovery, this direct method could be said to be an "action program"!

If we are standing as awareness now, what's the first thing we notice? There's apparently awareness here, and world over there. Forget for a moment about there being just one thing going on. That's ultimately true, of course, but that absolute viewpoint will limit our teaching tools right now. For the moment let us see that we are the *watcher*, not the watched; the *viewer*, not the viewed; the *seer*, not the seen; the *witness*, not the witnessed. We are the *single subject* to the bounteous and multifarious, objective world.

When we have taken our stand as pure awareness itself, then suddenly the oneness of our conceptual world can be clearly and easily seen as well. There are, I say with a wink, just "two things going on." This is the very highest level of duality, and it's a great and powerful step for us. We can look more deeply into the witness idea later, at our leisure. For now, let us revel in the freedom of clarity. The longer we look at the world in this way, the more different it gets. The ordinary becomes extraordinary; the mundane morphs into the sacred.

Remember several chapters back when we held our hands up so close to our faces that they were a blur? Then we slowly pulled them out until we could see them clearly. What was that lesson? "Very often," we said, "clarity comes with distance." The witness, sometimes called the *witness state*, gives us that valuable, initial distance. When the world is not *our* world, but instead it belongs to the character we're now watching, what happens in it is simply not so damn *personal*. It's not personal at all! And, look! It's *completely* fascinating. Look at that five star *dream*, would you! Wow! Look at the detail! Incredible! Sometimes I sit in my living room and actively drink in the world. Weather, walls, bookshelves, books. I open a book. Covers, chapter, pages—every one of them a concept. Paper, ink, words resting in a quiet sea of space; concepts swimming in concepts. Spine, head, tail, corner, gutter, endpaper, binding... oh! Who could ever make up such a thing? Who could ever spin such an amazing story?

You.

With this step we really begin to see and accept that there is just one thing going on, and thus just one amend to make, the imaginary split in ourselves. We come to see that it's an *imaginary* amend, but critical nonetheless. By working our way through the dark, we will surely come to the light. We can accept the provisional truth of the witness, and adopt it immediately, in everything we can: we apply it to thought and deed, to emotion and sensation. When we change the way we look at things, the things we look at change. It's that simple, and it's that powerful. It's a wonderful start for the wonderful journey from here to Here. We are now in a position to do as Jesus advised us when he said, "Physician, heal thyself."

In chapter nine we're going to present ways to help us see the healing truth about ourselves even more clearly. The way to do that is to simply chip away at ignorance, a little bit at a time. And that's just what we're going to do.

CHAPTER NINE
Step Nine

AMENDS

IN RECOVERY, THIS IS THE SCARIEST ACTION STEP OF THEM ALL. It entails us actually going out in the world to make amends for our wrongdoings. *Ouch.* A lot of people turn away from it. It's understandable. After making a single, effective amends, I also walked away from this step. That was back in 1983, seventeen years before I actually got clean and sober in a stable way. At least in my own mind I spent a lot of years all loaded up due to that omission. I've told many a man, "It's not an eight and a half step program. It's a *Twelve* Step program."

When we make our amend we look only at our part in whatever problem it was that caused us anger, fear, or any of the other seven deadly sins. Even if the other party was partially at fault—marginally, or majorly—we stick to where we feel we went astray, and hat in hand make our restitutions and apologies. This is *very* tough on ego, so even in a relative sense this step could be seen to be a Nondual movement. I haven't made amends to everyone I've ever harmed, but I made direct amends to those I harmed most, and I stand willing to make amends to the others.

Just a few months ago my wife and I were in a local bookstore when I saw a lawyer to whom I'd made an ugly comment some years ago. When I sobered up I realized I had not only been out of line, but that I'd made a fool out of myself. I'd misunderstood something he said, and lashed back with an ugly statement that had absolutely zero to do with the tabled discussion. It made as much sense as being served breakfast and attacking the waiter for not waking you up earlier. I burned over that for years, both in blame at what I'd said, and shame at my drunken bewilderment.

I walked up to the lawyer and introduced myself. He had no idea who I was. I told him what I'd done, and he didn't remember anything at all about it. I'd beaten myself up for years over something the victim couldn't even recall. He appreciated my gesture, however, and we struck up a conversation. We ended up wandering around the bookstore together, talking congenially. This is how a lot of amends work out. But not all.

My own diligent lawyer, who is now my great friend, wisely counsels that perhaps I should've given the amends process some additional thought back in 2000. I *certainly* understand his point of view! From a legal standpoint, what I did was suicide. Someone once asked me, concerning my amends and the ugliness that ensued, "If you knew then what you know now, would you still make those amends?" All I could say was, "I don't think it works that way." It makes my heart glad and light to know there is no such thing as "should." Everything happens the only way it can. Over and over I'm going to repeat that reality is *what is,* and there is no such thing as what isn't, including what might've, should've, or could've been in the past, and what might, should, and could happen in the future.

The ninth step can be pretty scary in the Nondual teaching outlined here, too, although it's completely different. You won't go to jail because of it, but just like in a court of law, you will be called upon to tell the truth. Jail might be easier! Regardless, it's time for us to make our amends, to wipe our rear-view mirror as clean as we can. In recovery we are dealing with others. In Nonduality it's been seen that there *are no* "others," not as seen from the absolute view. So amends in our case here means bringing our unconscious BOPs and patterns into the light of consciousness. It's not our job to get rid of them; it may be that they're a necessary part of the whole; we can't know. It's our job simply to bring them to the light and hold them there. Let me repeat that we are *not* trying to change a set of behaviors. That act in and of itself, well intentioned as it may be, is resistance decked out in a new party dress. It looks a lot better than it did before, but it still can't dance.

What we are doing is simply questioning and examining beliefs, opinions, and positions; we are looking into the nature of our BOPs. Behavior patterns that are tied to those may very well fall away of their own accord at some point, but that's really a side benefit. We are in search of truth, not polishing up what an idealized "me" should be like. Our patterns should be just like they are until they aren't. We could call *what is* by another name if we wished to: HDR, for high definition reality!

What we really want to see is *what happens*, and perhaps to ask, *why* this happens. When we look into "why," please note that we are using a relative tool for a relative exploration. The only real answer to a why question is, "Why not?" But here we're using dream tools to unveil the dream. We can't investigate reality, but we can investigate what's false. We are simply airing questions, and allowing our questioning *attitude* toward the highlighted belief—which is in turn tied to *all* of our other beliefs—to reverberate deeply. So we ask why in the spirit of knowing full well that, in a universe where there's only one thing going on, there actually *is no* specific causality. Everything causes everything else.

Here's a story that addresses what I mean. One afternoon a few years ago, within the bounds of a spiritual experience, reality presented itself to me by pulling back the make-believe curtain and showing itself as operating like a giant, mechanical clock-like thing, tick-tock-tick-tock, an entire universe in perfect harmony and symphony, without so much as a hair, or a breeze, or a fly's wing flaps unneeded or out of place. Everything looked like a sort of Sim City, if you're familiar with that computer game. On a more serious note, it was clear that any single movement was "empty" without all the supporting structure. And the supporting structure was itself "empty" without the myriad single movements. In unicity, where is either a whole or a part to be found?

This *clockness* experience was a translation of the way things are that I could readily understand, and accept without fear, and *grok* it on a deep, gut level. The universe was making a point, *presenting itself to itself* by using the dream tools at hand—a large burial ground, and a dream-insight for a pre-dead human unit we call Fred. To see a living metaphor of the world operating on this level is totally astonishing. That brief encounter moved me a long, long way. We can never unsee such a thing; it leaves a permanent ghost on our thinking. Nature has essentially *flashed* us!

In my case, that brief encounter was one of the most hilarious and enjoyable ten or fifteen minutes of my life. At the time—this occurred during a time when oscillation was still prevalent for me—it was a mighty encouragement to keep going the way I was going, and doing the things I was doing. We can't *expect* help like this, but that doesn't mean we won't get some that fits our own conditioning to a tee.

Let's get back to our step work. We can pull out our sheaf of papers, and pull from it a single sheet. One pattern at a time. We take steps to ensure that it is brought to the light, thus effectively making our amend.

We can't begin to identify unconscious BOPS or the behaviors they inspire—we can't "tell *on* ourselves, *to* ourselves"—unless we're first aware of that belief or behavior. What happens is that, with a proven willingness to bring unconscious patterns out of the closet, we'll find that the shingles fall from our eyes more often, and more quickly. Blind patterns begin to show themselves everywhere. Inquiry ends up taking up as much time as we'll lend to it, and goes on so long as we remain open. We actually have to wake up in order to find out just how *unawake* our me-ness has been and still remains. Only upon awakening do we find out we've been in a full coma! Regardless of what we might hear to the contrary, it's my experience, and the experience of many teachers I've talked to and read, that only upon awakening does the real work begin. So-called enlightenment may be the end of one apparent process, but it is surely the beginning of another.

This uncovering is not a quick and easy process, and it's not pretty. For me, however poorly I may embody awakeness, this inquiry has nonetheless taken over and become an active, ongoing part of life. I remind you that I started this thing while standing in quite a deep hole, so I can make an awful lot of progress and still not be much to brag about. Inquiry essentially becomes continuous, although the questions change dramatically. Even the thought, "Okay, that's the last one," meaning the last pattern or blockage of ignorance or arrogance that needs to be seen through, is in fact only the *newest and freshest* blockage of ignorance and arrogance that will have to be seen through *next*! We're never ever *done*. We need to get over even wanting to be done, because that, too, will hold us back.

It's so funny that there's so much emphasis on "being done." Perhaps this is a particularly American failing, but I doubt it. I went through that longing, and may go through it again later today—I can't know. But other than ego, who would really *give a damn* about "being done"? So far as I can tell we *start out* "being done," being sure, knowing it all, and the entire point of the spiritual process is about coming *undone*, about becoming *unsure*, and then existing undone, unsure, unknowing all the way into *right now*!

A taken opportunity to see through our beliefs, opinions, and positions breeds another opportunity to do so, like replicating links in a chain. We have to *want* to know, and given that we, as addicts, are experts in the practice of denial, this can be easier said than done. Any of us might glom onto a thought and believe it ten seconds from now; who knows? All it takes is one. Any thought will do. If we think, "Okay, *now* I'm finally enlightened," it automatically means we're *not*. We might use such language in passing, but we would never use it as a pretense of truth. However, let me also quickly point out that thinking the opposite way, "Okay, I see that trap, and I'm coming around behind it—I'm *not* enlightened!" doesn't secretly mean, "I tricked the universe—and *now* I'm done."

I am sitting at my desk laughing out loud. If one can back up from the seeming seriousness of it all, the whole "school of done," is absolutely hilarious! "I'm done! No, I'm not done! Hey, is it over yet? Damn, I don't think I'm done! Is *she* done? Is *he*? Are we there yet? Oh shit, have we secretly been *un*done? Where in the hell do we *go* to finish?"

We want to embrace the idea of continuous work through the continuing character we think we are until we don't. We want to remember what was said earlier: enlightenment—simply seeing things as they are—is all about right now. We are awake to *this* moment and its content, or we are not. A spiritual experience that came and went five years ago, or yesterday afternoon, or what we knew or saw five minutes, ago doesn't matter. Am I living in truth *right now*? Nothing else counts.

Living in inquiry is the counterbalance to thinking we "have" something. It always brings us back to this situation, to this moment, and to questioning this assumption. It requires more humility than I am sometimes willing to offer, but then I suffer and get flexible again. Thus suffering becomes our friend, because it's the alarm clock in the dream. If we are experiencing personal suffering, then we are asleep to at least what's causing that. Perhaps we're awake to many other things—I mean this absolutely sincerely—but we're asleep to anything that's causing us suffering.

I have to jump in here and establish that I'm not saying we, as apparent individuals *shouldn't* suffer. We *do* suffer. There is suffering all over the world, suffering as we cannot even adequately imagine. Suffering *is*. See how simple this is? To believe that we *shouldn't* suffer when we *do* suffer is to... *suffer*! If I felt like it should be otherwise, then I'd take that idea into inquiry and see if it made any sense. If it didn't make any sense for me to continue fighting the *isness* of suffering, if I saw it wasn't beneficial, and I saw that *clearly*, then people would continue to suffer, but I wouldn't be joining them, at least about *that*. There would still be plenty of other opportunities for me to pout over until I dealt with them. But I would be enlightened to at least the single bogus idea that people shouldn't suffer.

Enlightenment is not escape from suffering or anything else. It is the willingness to accept whatever comes. Suffering is part of *what is* for us until it isn't. Enlightenment isn't even *about* us! It's not *for* us. We, I remind you, only exist under certain conditions. All of those conditions fall *within* enlightenment. As crazy as it sounds, enlightenment is for itself. If that doesn't make sense right now, that's okay. The odds are good that one day it will.

What we're really talking about, when we discuss the end of suffering in a Nondual way, is the end of personalized, psychological suffering. If the personal me is seen through, if that concept is seen to be false, it drops. In the absence of a personal me, who is there to suffer? There is still *suffering*, but there's no one doing it. We are no longer confusing ourselves as being a single, solitary human being, and thus *we* don't suffer. I'm saying "we" for the sake of literary flow, but whenever I say we, I actually mean "I." I mean "I," because, as we know, and as we're hopefully beginning to internalize, there *really is* just one thing going on.

More on this suffering notion. We can be functioning as wakefulness and still be in a hell of a lot of physical pain, or feeling deep, emotional grief, but we can't *simultaneously* be wakefulness and be suffering psychologically. We are 100% one way or 100% the other; we are in or we are out. For *now*! To *this*! Based on firsthand knowledge, I can tell you that we can *at least* reach a place where resistance ceases to come very often, and when it does, it's not for long. I'm still fully capable of resisting *what is*. But once it's seen that an imaginary Fred is resisting an imaginary condition, then that resistance usually drops back into the ocean of acceptance.

If one of our cats died, I would certainly grieve. Grieving would naturally arise out of that situation. I certainly wouldn't try to resist that. We can actually grieve without suffering; they are not the same thing. Grief can also spring from gratitude. I point this out simply for the sake of keeping our thinking wide open.

Even great sages have reported the persistence of, in their cases, instant on-and-off vacillation. It's no big deal. In the rooms we say, "We are not saints," which lets us off the hook for being human. Here let's say, "We are not great sages," and let ourselves off the hook for what happens, instead of suffering from the wishing we were "more enlightened" than we are.

If stand-down doesn't happen automatically immediately, as is sometimes the case with me, then inquiry will bring us back to earth, to reality, every time. Living in inquiry is not something we *think* about doing long-term, though we will probably think about it for quite a while. At some point, however, we begin to notice ourselves questioning our BOPs and behaviors automatically. We may first see it almost as a lovely novelty. But at some point it morphs into something that just happens. Inquiry does itself. It's another part of life that is taken care of *for* us, like our breathing, hair and nails, and blood flow. If that's not a thousand percent correct, it's pretty durn close.

For five years I spent countless hours sitting in my living room—thinking, reflecting, and doing inquiry—with a pen and one yellow legal pad after another, exploring my beliefs, opinions, and positions, and the behaviors they engendered. I really wanted to know the truth, even if I disagreed with it. I borrowed some investigatory methods from other teachers, and invented some of my own. The method I'm presenting here, The BOP Inquiry, is sort of a conglomeration of those. It's simple, easy, it can prove helpful quickly, and I've found it effective. I still use it. It still works. The great thing is that when mind really sees the truth about something, it stops arguing with it. It'll go argue with something else, but it'll be quiet on that issue. And slowly the still pool expands.

Let me backpedal just a little here before we go into our methodology. Expecting a Higher Power to *override* our conscious unwillingness to seek truth, thus allowing us to sidestep the uncomfortable work of self-discovery, is probably not going to work for us. While it apparently does happen, it occurs so rarely that it's not even worth our addressing. The last *complete* override I can recall was when Saul of Tarsus was stricken blind and almost molecularly reformed on the road to Damascus. Of course I'm sure to have missed some miracles in the ensuing two thousand years, but I wouldn't waste time holding out for one of my own. Nonetheless, this holding out is a popular path because, although it typically *delivers* nothing, it requires nothing on our part, and we can pretend that this "waiting for God" is actual activity and not just the laziness and denial—or at best ignorance—that is typically being covered up.

We're going to use as our classroom inquiry an all-too-common example of unconsciousness *literally* at the wheel: road rage. I don't know how prevalent this is in the rest of the world, but in the U. S. it's all too common, and it's a really serious problem. Here's how Wikipedia defines it: "Road rage is an aggressive or angry behavior by a driver of an automobile or other motor vehicle. Such behavior might include rude gestures, verbal insults, deliberately driving in an unsafe or threatening manner, or making threats. Road rage can lead to altercations, assaults, and collisions which result in injuries and even deaths."

I hate to think that people are dying over missed turn signals, but they are. I've heard this war pattern talked about in loads of recovery meetings, and I see it happening fairly regularly in traffic. I used to have a bad case of it myself, but that movement hasn't shown its face around here in quite a while. That doesn't mean it *won't*, and I can't brag on what I didn't do to begin with, but it's a relief to not have it regularly eating my peacefulness—and threatening the peacefulness of others—the way it used to. Here's a good example of road rage in action that I personally witnessed.

Years ago I watched a pickup truck deliberately broadside and smash a car, running it completely off an interstate highway in Charlotte, North Carolina. Both of the cars were going about eighty miles per hour when this occurred. I know, because I was doing eighty or so, and I was at one point just to the right of the offender, and just behind the victim. I was also a hothead at the time, and wasn't going to miss any opportunity to go to war. Without going into all of that, I'll tell you that since I was stupid enough to get involved, I found out what had happened prior to my witnessing this attempted murder.

All of this began ostensibly because the driver of the car "cut in front of" the driver of the truck. The driver's error in judgment was taken to be an insult and a threat by the truck driver. Beyond all reason, that common, albeit discourteous driving faux pas, on that day, fell into the truck driver's category of "capital offense." He'd been *dissed* as the kids says, and so the *disser* should die! It's unthinkable to us, but somebody thought this very thing, and acted on it, and damn near killed a promising young man as a result.

Whether it threatens us physically or not, and regardless of if we're the sender or the receiver of it, this kind of blind rage is perilous to our state of mind, and at least temporarily devastating to any apparent spiritual progress. Like everything else, it leaves a footprint. And it's not something we can simply dismiss as a destined-by-heaven "character defect," nor do we get to just wink and nod and refer to ourselves as being "a work in progress." Not, that is, if we're on a sincere spiritual path.

If we're really going to try and take the spiritual train as far as the tracks run, then we don't get to pick and choose where we're going to surrender, and where we're going to resist. A hard position against anything is a soft position against everything. No matter what we're resisting, it's the same personalized me-ness that's *doing* the resisting, and by allowing this to pass unexamined, we keep that very same apparent me-ness embodied and thriving. The fuel feeds the fire, and the hotter fire burns, the better it dries surrounding fuel to feed itself. There's no end to it. Yes, we've already noted that we may be clearer in some areas than others, but our underlying goal is still to actively root out unconsciousness wherever we find it. Our ultimate paradoxical goal may be to "let go of letting go," but at this stage, simply letting go of what doesn't work for us is a damn fine move in that direction. You can't let go of a thing if you're sitting on your hands.

So, let us go to our investigation. We take our notebook and pen, and we sit down and begin to look closely into our road rage. If you're afflicted with this, then it shouldn't be difficult to bring an example up in memory. If you're not, and never have been, I still don't think it will be too terribly difficult to imagine. Whether the incident is fresh, old, or imaginary doesn't matter so long as we can mentally relive it *now*.

Pretend someone has just cursed at us, threatened us, waved a fist in our faces, or laid on their horn in our direction. Immediately, unthinkingly, we are struck, steamed, insulted; moving up the temper scale from cool, to hot, to boiling within just a fraction of a second. Who *is* this attacker? What on earth are they doing? *Why* are they doing it? The reckless fools! *Idiots*, no less! Who do they think they are? Do they not know who *we* are?

And on and on and on.

Did you ever wonder how a total stranger can find a hot button so fast? It's because our hot buttons are not passive; they are *hunters*. They are ever on the prowl for hurt or harm, slight or insult. They'll throw a victim's emotional hooks into any form of aggravation in order to better hold it and own it. Ego is restless, irritable, and discontent, and will never completely rest, because for it to rest is for it to die. Thus we find ourselves in a permanent state of undeclared war. You could say that we are "warring waiting to declare itself," always identifying potential opponents, ever calculating the degree of fear and anger required to meet them and match them. Oddly enough, winning and losing is completely secondary! The real game is the constant fueling of the illusion of the separate me, which by the very nature of its existence is continually under threat. Threat is its life blood. Victor or victim, it's all the same to ego. The dream of separation gives birth to hot buttons like a spider gives birth to babies—in endless droves. We set our hot buttons out like pickets to guard our perimeter, with directions to shoot first and ask questions later. Sooner or later, you can bet that something will cross our lines, especially since our lines are in continuous outward movement, always in search of a border clash.

When we find opposition we immediately *react out*—strongly. What do we do? In the case of this other driver's road rage, we fight fire with more fire. We curse and yell back, we raise *our* fists, flip *our* fingers, we lay down on *our* horn. In short, we mirror our assailant. Monkey see, monkey do, all without a decision, all within a tightly woven pattern. There is just *activity happening*. There is no conscious individual even present at the scene. Conscious awareness is on holiday at the Mediterranean, and these patterns on both sides are running entirely *on their own*. These patterns need fuel, but they don't need a manager; they do the managing, or the mismanaging, all by themselves—at everyone's expense.

A stranger's hot button was hit, via a random car swerving in front of him in a random event, and nearly causing a random accident. But the first driver is *compelled* to make it all about him, so in our perfect mirroring way, we are, in turn, *compelled* to make it all about us. The first driver's personalization of the event set off a defensive-aggressive blind pattern, which in turn hit another hot button—ours. We now personalize the other driver's *reacting-out*, which sets off our own defensive-aggressive blind pattern. Think of this scene as being like a ghostly pinball machine, where lights are flashing and bells are ringing, but no one pulled the plunger, there's no one at the flippers, and there's no one keeping score. The machine is playing itself. Both drivers ultimately "win," because both identities are firmed up by way of victimship, by being sure, and right, and righteous, and by the aggressive actions they took to defend themselves. But in truth, it all just *happened*. The universal was made to look personal. The accidental was made to look purposeful. The unconscious was made to look thoughtful. No one was even there, but you can *bet* that at least two stories were born out of it.

Every hot button is connected to a livewire, and at the other end of that livewire you will always find a fixed *belief, opinion, or position*, what I call a BOP. Each of these "BOPs" is a self-identifier. They are ultimately what make up a separate me. In the absence of BOPs, what do you have? *What is*. What else? Nothing. This is why we're not so keen to be rid of our buttons, or their underlying beliefs, opinions, or positions, although we often declare that we are. We have to be at quite a serious stage in our spiritual development before we will take this dismantling job on because, deep down, we know the truth: no buttons, no BOPs, no "me." In the absence of that resistance, there is no individual presence left over. *What is* rules.

To make it as clear as I can, what I am saying here is that we, the theoretical individual, are not "resistant"; we are, in fact, *resistance itself*. The story of me that we take to be separate and real is a fiction that is *composed* of resistance. Our day to day experience, what we casually and erroneously refer to as "reality," is built on separation—me and my world; what I do like, and what I don't like; what I want more of, and what I want less of; what I want to happen, and what I want to stop happening; what should be going on, and what shouldn't be going on; what might have been, and what might yet be—which neatly cuts out *any* room for *right now* or *what is*. Our identity is constructed around contrasting opposites that appear to flow in an endless stream, seemingly arriving from somewhere and heading to somewhere else, with a more or less static "me" apparently cast in between. It's just not true.

That *is* the dream. The dream stream isn't coming from one place and heading to another, although there is certainly *streamness*. The streamness isn't even really flowing, at least not in the conventional sense. It *appears* to be flowing. And the "me-ness" I think I see is simply an appearance within an appearance, a reflection on the still waters; it is, in fact, part and parcel of the streamness. There is just one thing going on, with no opposites, which is completely timeless and unmoving. I don't even know *what* it is, but I know that whatever it is, *it is*.

We're not after intellectual knowledge here, but we use the mind to go beyond the mind, and even an intellectual grasp of what's being said here has value; it can bring a certain sense of relief and, more importantly, it be used as the leading edge of a wedge that when driven home can and will ultimately wake us up. But for most of us, it must be *driven home* by actual investigation and inquiry, and we are best served to put that inquiry down on paper. This helps keep us on point, keep us honest, and it aids in making us at least somewhat *more* objective about ourselves, though of course that's too much of a stretch to ever declare victory on.

The methodology I employ in this book is one that's been worked out over the years in my living room. I offer it to you as a guide. If you like it, fine; use it. If you don't, that's fine as well. Find another. Invent your own. My sense with inquiry is the same as my sense was in taking and guiding people through the Twelve Steps: *intent* is far more important than *form*. In recovery I've seen a lot of people get hung up on form, and completely forget their intent! And then get loaded. Here, we're trying to find out the truth about ourselves; to unloose blind patterns; to unravel and unwind our story; and to begin dismantling the dream of me-ness *from within the dream itself.* We use the mind to help transcend the mind. Find your own way. There are teachers out there with excellent systems of inquiry that a lot of people have found to be successful. Seek them out. Find out what works for *you.* This is an intensely individual practice. I'm just saying that this is how *I* do it.

Excercise 8: The BOP Inquiry

✳

We can start with either a statement, or a question. I use whichever arises first. Either way, I like it to be bold, firmly upholding our point of view, even skewing it in our favor. We want to set down hard, sharp lines that will be easy to spot when we cross them.

Our *opening statement* might be, **"I am always a good driver."** An *opening question* we could use in place of our statement is, **"Why can't they see I'm a good driver?"**

This is our operational story line, and it was this story line—in our old, recent, or invented example—that we felt was being attacked by the other driver. We, as separate individuals, are composed of multiple story lines, all of which can be turned a special way in the light of inquiry, so that we can see clearly that they are all simply resistance wearing a lot of different hats. A monkey with a hat on is still a monkey. Ultimately, resistance can be found at the core of all beliefs, opinions, and positions, because there's a "me" in there that's holding them, and that me-ness is resistance in action. The BOPs are the me's minions in the world. Behaviors are just the part of the dance we see, like the strings waving in front of a fan. You may be able to stop those strings by seduction or coercion, but if you don't cut off the fan, they're going to wave again just as soon as we let go of them.

Notice that the way we've framed our statement or question that we're tightly cornered right from go. Our strongest story lines are always black and white and only begin to yield a bit of gray upon close examination. Now, in the spirit of honest inquiry, we come back and ask ourselves if our statement is really true, or if our question's theme even holds water. Are we really always good drivers? Is there evidence to back that up? Is there evidence to the contrary? What can we present to prove that our statement is true? Can we think of any instance where that *wasn't* true? Are we a habitual drunkard driving with a suspended license? This last would be an example of our question's theme not even holding water, which would thereby save us a lot of time!

We have twin objectives here. One is to bring our patterns, and our defenses of those patterns out of the shadows. The second is to introduce doubt. We could say that doubt is itself another form of light. We want to find out if our existing beliefs, opinions, and positions are true. We want to find out if our defenses of them are rational, or if they're just based on other BOPs, like Russian Matryoshka dolls with a whole set of nesting, wooden figures, one lying inside another. BOPs nest within each other in just that same way.

We have to be careful in our investigation, which means we have to remain rigorously honest. Otherwise we end up using the inquiry process to simply back up what we were already feeling, and legitimize our false stand. In that case, we use more lies to cover up the first batch of lies, and end up worse off than ever. This is a pattern most addicts know all too well. We do this unconsciously all the time. Let's consciously avoid doing it here.

Here's an example of a false *transitional statement*: "**I haven't had a ticket in twenty years.**" When a defensive statement arises, we can't just give it a cursory inspection to see if it's true and call it good. It's critical that the *spirit* of the statement be true to our purpose. If we haven't had a ticket in twenty years, is that because we have driven perfectly for more than 7,000 days, or because *we didn't get caught* when we drove *less than* perfectly? Please. Who hasn't run a yellow light that went red? Who hasn't broken the speed limit, changed lanes improperly, or made a turn without giving a signal? For any of us, the lack of a ticket for two decades is simply great luck; it's just because we didn't get caught. Granted, it may also be indicative that we are good and safe drivers *most* of the time, and that's wholly terrific, but that's a far cry from being a good and safe driver *all* the time. How, for instance, was our driving *earlier today*, when the road rage incident got set off? Our "no ticket" statement was trying to circumnavigate the truth by *bypassing* the spirit of our inquiry. We might say such a thing to ourselves and get away with it, but if we've got it on paper it'll almost surely look hollow.

A truer *transitional statement*, meaning a statement where I am really trying to unearth the dark, might be something like, **"I am a good driver most of the time."** That "most" looms large as a happy signal of doubt. Thus, so long as this is an accurate statement, it's not necessarily defensive. It's just a flat fact, with an undertone of honest doubt. But we can also see that it doesn't really leave us much of an opening to work with. It's the distinct opening that is the key. So, as we said earlier, let's turn it around in the light and see if there is another way to say the same thing that might be more in line with our purpose. We're looking for something which is just as accurate, and yet is *looser*, thereby providing us with a *handle*, so to speak.

"Sometimes I am not a good driver." *Now* we are starting to tell ourselves the real truth, and we are doing so within the spirit of being honest with ourselves. Sometimes we are a good driver, and sometimes we're not. I think it's fair to say this is a near-universal truth. So, now that we've broken the spell of our supposed superior driving skills, in reference to the *specific situation* that brought us into this inquiry to begin with, what might be even closer to the truth? We've moved in slowly, but we've moved in steadily; let's try again.

"I was not a good driver today." *Here's* a pay dirt acknowledgement. Whether what the other guy did was wise or called for is not ours to ask or answer. We're not working on the other driver; we're working on us. In recovery we would say that we are "taking our own inventory" and not the other person's. Now that we've told *on* ourselves, *to* ourselves, ego's balloon is beginning to shrink. It's hard to be angry at someone who was upset by our own screw-up. Yes, they re-acted out, but they had a valid reason: we scared them! We reacted out, too, and *we* didn't have a valid reason. If we use our own yardstick on ourselves, then we were simply being defensive for the *sake* of being defensive. If we really want to make our point, we'll carry on from here. It's not enough for us to simply see the truth, or not in my opinion. In practice, when I do this, I just go ahead and mash my nose into it. Clearly we don't do this from the standpoint of guilt, shame, or blame, but when we *overkill* a thing, we *do* tend to notice it.

"The other driver was right." Don't you just *hate* this overkill? Doesn't it burn? Ouch! But isn't it more true than our opening set of BOPs? Those didn't burn, because we weren't seen as being at fault. Now I'm simply stating that the other driver was right, and that my opening statement or question was hogwash. If I then want to offload a bunch of feel-bad crap from that statement onto myself, I can. It's available. But I certainly don't *have* to, and clearly it wouldn't be my suggestion. I can just *acknowledge* that the other driver was right. That does indeed make us wrong, but it doesn't make us terminally *bad*.

Let me say again that this is not a driving lesson. If you happen to end up a better driver, swell, but that's not our point. The original Twelve Steps can probably help you with that kind of thing. Here, if you end up a *clearer human*, then we have succeeded. The good news, however, is that when we unwind these untrue and unhelpful beliefs, opinions, and positions, the behaviors that inspired them do tend to begin to fade. A boat without an anchor will drift. And a boat with a hole in it will *sink*. I stress that this is a byproduct. Going after behaviors rather than BOPs may leave us with more deeply ingrained behaviors, and more nesting Matryoshka figures. When I do this, I won't pretend there's *zero* alternative motive, but there's very little. We do the best we can.

Let's pound this thing just a little more. If we splatter it, maybe it will be unable to stand!

"Why do I try to protect my bad behaviors?" This is one of those great *why* questions we talked about earlier. We don't have an answer. There *isn't* an answer. We can also point to our BOPs and ask, **"Why do I have [this specific] belief, opinion, or position that leads me to protect my bad behaviors?"** Use what works for you. What works is the unchallenged ruler of this kingdom. If you think you need to go into something specific, go into it, but we're not looking for answers, we're looking for the experience of spaciousness that's left in the void of our *inability* to answer!

Other questions we might use are, **"Why would I get angry at a stranger who was pointing out a flaw in me?"** We can come up with a long list of them, but two or three will do. One more we could use is, **"What makes me think I own the road?"**

Let's look now at some *cost statements*. For everything there is a price, and that includes allowing entrenched BOPs to remain. Without any change in our BOPs or behavior, can we see what this price might be? Here I would simply use a list. Back in the days when I was a salesman, there was something known as the "Benjamin Franklin close." This was supposed to close the sale via helping the customer use logic to make a decision as to whether he or she should buy our offering or not. You take a piece of paper and draw a line down the middle. On the left-hand side you write down every reason that a positive decision would be a good thing. In the case of a car, for instance, that list might contain things like safety, fuel economy, enhanced self-esteem, no repair bills, attracting the opposite sex, pleasing the family, whatever comes up for us. The salesman *helps* the customer come up with as many reasons to buy as they can; the more the better.

When it comes to the right-hand side of the list, the salesman doesn't help the customer. They're left on their own, and they have to come up with their own reasons. Quite often the customer can come up with only one item: it's too expensive. You have them write that down. It looks rather lost amid the cluster of go-ahead reasons. The set-up for the closing question here is, "Mr. Customer, under 'Reasons For Buying' you've put down a whole lot of very good reasons why this purchase would be good for you and your family." Here the salesman might read some or all of them out—in a helpful manner, of course! Then he'll continue with his question. "On the other side, under 'Reasons Against Buying,' you've only got one thing written down, and that's price. We both know you can afford this new car if you want to. Can I go ahead and tell them to wash it up for you?"

It's a deadly close. I've had it used on *me*, when I knew what the guy was doing, and I still ended up becoming a buyer.

We are essentially doing the same thing here. The idea here is to let ourselves see the very practical price of continuing to cover up a deeper clarity. Again and again, we're not beating ourselves up, we're just *noticing*. We can take it to the extreme; we can even be funny. What matters is that we *notice*.

Our *set-up statement* for our list might be, "If I continue to cover up my driving deficiencies with defensive reacting-out, instead of accepting the goddamn helpful driving tips other drivers are going out of their way to share with me, I could, practically speaking:

"Get a ticket and break my glowing, twenty-year record.

"Have a wreck.

"Get killed.

"Cripple or kill somebody else.

"Kill a child.

"Knock over a school bus.

"End up going to jail."

We'd use the same statement above for the "spiritual side" of things, and our list might look something like:

"I might go *backward* on the spiritual track.

"Never learn to be honest.

"Stay confused.

"Remain in suffering.

"Stay in fear.

"Keep getting angry.

"Never get enlightened."

There's no one to tell us when our list is complete. We'll know. I've done them with three examples, and I've done them with thirty, depending on the nature of the behavior and the BOPs. I wouldn't accept anything less than three as being honest work. And I'd write until I was out of examples.

Our final step here involves issuing our *evolutionary statements*. Please recall what I said earlier. I'm setting all this up with statements and steps, because it's the way of books. What I'm really trying to transfer is simply a *zeal* for the truth. If we adapt that zeal, the rest will come, and form be damned.

At any rate, evolutionary statements are generalities that we've picked up on as we've worked with our specific problem. In this case they might be:

"Sometimes I defend myself when I'm in the wrong.

"Some things I believe about myself aren't true.

"I may not always know what's going on."

These are three fresh, freeing doubts we didn't have when we entered this inquiry, because we didn't even know these patterns existed. It's wonderful stuff for our arsenal. Just seeing these and putting them down on paper will cause them to act like little Pac Man figures that go about gnawing at the edges of our oh-so-sure thinking. When we begin unwinding our patterns, we begin unwinding our world-in-the-head. When we start unwinding the world-in-our-head, we start to unravel ourselves—actually to unravel the *story* of ourselves, which is all that me-ness and we-ness ever are. And then, if we're lucky or blessed, we are shown experientially that that's all there ever was to us—story. The cliff is removed from our feet.

Afterwards, we still find out that even with the main acts dismantled, there are lots and lots of little acts and actions and stories that continued inquiry can help us uncover and unleash.

Uncovering is our job. Results really are none of our business. If you have adopted a zeal for digging in the dark, this method of inquiry can be adapted to fit virtually any set of BOPs surrounding any set of behaviors, feelings, whatever. There's no need for me to take this example any further. At this stage it's a do-it-to-yourself program.

In recovery they sometimes talk about the H.O.W. of the cleaning up process, which comes down to Honesty, Openness, and Willingness. We especially want to bring those same qualities here. If we do that, ultimately we cannot fail. The single most important thing anyone can apparently do to hasten an apparent awakening is to be willing to drop what they know, or think they know—including, perhaps even *especially*, what they know or think they know about spirituality.

I also want to say that it's good to keep in mind that awareness is always already awake. What this inquiry is doing is apparently *unwrapping* it, one sheet of paper at a time. So enlightenment is available—it's *waiting* for us, so to speak—with every inquiry session, and even with every question. The same can be said about each specific topic we look into. This inquiry process *may* take us some time, but it certainly doesn't *have* to. Enlightenment is available to everyone on this planet with every breath, at every moment. This is a process of unhooking. If we follow our thoughts back to what we're unhooking *from*, and see that clearly, then our search is over. We'll have discovered the truth by having seen the false.

But of course, as we've already said, it's never over; that's just a manner of speaking. I'm sure you know what Zen monks say about enlightenment. "Before enlightenment, chopping wood, carrying water. After enlightenment, chopping wood, carrying water." In a similar fashion we can say, "Before awakening, inquiry. After awakening, inquiry." Inquiry is a good friend and a trustworthy companion for our spiritual journey. It's a fine way to make amends to ourselves, and heal our apparent separation.

With the satisfactory completion of the ninth step, at least in regard to this text, we have reached the end of the action steps. We could say that the end of this movement perfectly prepares us for what are known as the three "maintenance" steps. That's where we're heading next.

CHAPTER TEN
Step Ten

INTEGRITY

IN THE RECOVERY TRADITION, THE TENTH STEP IS ABOUT TAKING A continuing inventory, and promptly admitting where we were wrong. There's little need for translation here. The two traditions of recovery and Nonduality meet firmly here; if not in method, then certainly in intent. The idea behind this movement, whether viewed through the eyes of recovery or Nonduality, is one of continuous *integrity*, and implies an ongoing vigilance. In recovery we're keeping a sharp eye open for what we call "old behavior." It's always about self-centeredness, no matter what hat self-centeredness might be wearing on that day: greed, lust, sloth; fill in the blank with your own favorite deadly sin.

Vigilance in Nondualism, however, can conjure up an idea of *intensity* that doesn't really apply, or certainly not in the way it's presented here. "Working really hard at staying awake"—at embodiment, at living our realization—is generally *not* going to prove successful. This "worker bee" school of thought is more likely to prove successful in keeping us *asleep*, because the problem that arises in the face of all that efforting, the inner declaration that "I'm going to do this right no matter what," is that it tends to harden our sense of an egoic core. We don't want to confuse intensity with earnestness. Intensity springs from *will*, where earnestness springs from *willingness*.

Yet we know that on the other side of things, what we might call the "couch potato" school of awakening, the "there's nothing to do and no one to do it," nobody-no-method *method*, unless we're exceptionally blessed, is probably going to prove futile. It happens, but not in large numbers, and I remind you that here we are aiming to use the Law of Large Numbers to aid us in finding the most efficient path—for *us*. One of the problems with any method, even the no-method method, is that ego is always happy—and generally busy—rebuilding itself out of the materials on hand, which very much includes the glistening spiritual story.

So if we're not worker *beeing*, and we're not *potatoing*, what is it that we're to do? I suggest that for us this movement is really about balance, about an *alert relaxation* into the paradoxical understanding that our work is always *done*, yet never *fully* done; that our current seeing-being is what matters; and that rigorous honesty and humility within the present moment must remain our paramount interest. *Interest*, however, is a far cry from the extremes of disregard or worry. And of course it's easier said than done. Allowing our spiritual story to naturally unfold while still keeping a sharp eye on ourselves is surely walking the razor's edge. We can take comfort in knowing that many have walked it before us, and are doing so even now. If they can do it, so can we; we know they're no better or worse than us, because there's only one thing going on.

What many seekers will eventually do is hook up with a living teacher, and often enough a surrounding group. This can be an excellent move. Some find it nearly impossible to succeed alone, thus joining a group is an easier, softer way to remain vigilant. It's also comforting, because perhaps for the first time in a long time we feel like we *really* fit in. We make friends and connections, and share a common bond, a bond which is the deepest one available in the relative world.

All that's great. But there can be an underside to the spiritual search, and that's what we want to discuss here. It's not altogether comfortable, but I do think it's vital to at least mention it.

Ego loves a spiritual story, because it's laced with both power and elitism. The only thing better than being special is being *doubly* special. It's very tricky territory to tread. Thus if we're not careful we attach to a spiritual view of, and story about, ourselves. When we do, we end up being like the Texan who is "all hat and no cows:" we look spiritual, we talk spiritual, we have spiritual friends, we take spiritual vacations (called retreats), and we even act spiritual—whatever that means—but we're still asleep to our true nature. A wise basic notion to keep in mind is that, in a world where there is only one thing going on, what is either spiritual, or unspiritual? What is, in the deepest sense, either esoteric or exoteric; sacred or secular? Reality is bigger than all of those, and it *includes* all of it.

On the more relative side of things, perhaps we've made a lot of progress since we began our journey. That's great, I'm all for it. I'm certainly not the person to criticize any practical or spiritual progress, improved citizenship, or deepening sense of connection to either a group or a Higher Power. All of that is absolutely fine and commendable. But let's do be absolutely clear that all such progress is occurring to a character in a play. The events within any play, including the one we call "our life," which is a misnomer, are important *in relationship to the play as a whole.* But what about *outside* of the play, *beyond* the play? How about the most important thing that can happen to us? How about actual *liberation*? Are the teacher and group moving us toward that, or are we stagnating in the surrounding social scene? I don't pretend that liberation is for everyone; it's not. The question to ask yourself is, "Is it for *me*?" If it is, then we want to check ourselves closely. The road to the Gateless Gate is littered with the ghosts of those whose intentions were good, but whose integrity was not strong enough to make the long journey.

Please, let's not do a 180 here. I'm not saying there is anything wrong with spiritual groups, retreats, beautiful clothing, incense, or other spiritual trappings. I'm fond of them myself. Parts of my home look like an Asian bazaar. I like that stuff; I've had a house full of it for thirty years, so I'm far more guilty than most. We just want to make sure, no matter what trappings we indulge in, that we keep our hearts open, and our eyes on the real prize, not the booby prizes that litter the way to self-realization.

This brushes up against the idea of practical integrity, which is very reminiscent of the recovery path, so let's touch on that while we're here. I wish I could tell you that so-called enlightenment was a guarantee of sound thinking and good behavior. It's not. In the rooms we talk about the fact that if you sober up a drunken horse thief, then you're left with a sober horse thief. Recovery understands this idea of incremental growth very, very well.

We can have a glimpse, or even an apparent long experience, of our true nature and later—not even *much* later—go wildly off course. I saw it happen in me. I still see unconscious judgments and behavior playing through, some subtle, some less so. It's about a thousand percent better than it was, but it's not gone yet. I should also confess here, just for the sake of the clear example, that I was an enlightened ego for two or three *years* after I woke up, which is a long time for friends and family to bear someone who's in that mode. Most of them did.

What I mean by an enlightened ego is that you've gone from seeker to seer to knower. Seeker is innocent and just fine. Seer is grace and great. Knower is death. Some people never get out of it. I see it happening now in a couple of teachers I've had dealings with in the last year. I suspect they'll wake up to themselves again, but one can't know. It's a good thing to be aware of, and to keep in the back of our minds as we move away from solitary study and practice, and out into the larger world. There are teachings out there specifically designed to help you with that if you keep your eyes and ears open to them. It takes some humility, which is why it took me so long. Humility has never been my strong suit, although I can have it beaten into me.

What we can be sure of is that the current, *living* experience of awakeness does indeed foster good citizenry and sound, compassionate behavior. What we would call poor citizenry and lousy behavior patterns always stem from a sense of separation, a central point of reference, a "me." Awakeness has no such point, and thus it has no such problems. I wanted to touch on this, but now let's return to our discussion of the other forms of spiritual integrity.

Mind is always looking for a way and a place to pull a fast 180. We've talked about the unstable and unreal nature of 180 degree spiritual movements before, and we'll explore it in a little more detail here. The mind can't be blamed; this off and on, zero and one, movement is its nature, and the nature of duality itself. Every peak has its requisite matching valley. So mind loves to jump from one pole to the next, because there is always apparent security within extremity. There may not be much in the way of *accuracy or thoughtfulness* in an extreme position, but there is certainly a lot of *sureness and security*. Held within the warm embrace of an extremity, ego is not only right, it's dead right, absolutely right, *inarguably* right. Ego, as we talked about in the last chapter, now finds itself unrelentingly *sure*. This is not a healthy, loving, or honest place for us to be.

The spiritual search is not immune to this movement toward extremities. In fact, I think it fair to say that the spiritual search is especially *prone* to this movement, because most of us enter the spiritual search only upon having experienced an extreme valley, a sense of personal failure like disaster, depression, dread, some other equally devastating blow. In my case there was also the addition of an entire life lived rashly and particularly unskillfully. And of course, most of us here experienced addiction, which can certainly foster plenty of disaster, depression and dread all on its own.

Once we become seekers, then it's easy to see ourselves as problems in search of an answer. And therein lies the rub. Once we connect with other human beings on a deep spiritual level—which typically means a core, trusting, *primal* level—then in the absence of unrelenting integrity on both parties' behalf, we can find ourselves in one of those self-reinforcing feedback loops we talked about earlier. Our world can get smaller instead of larger. And when we then connect with others who believe the same things we do, who are conducting their lives in a similar fashion, and hold similar personal and planetary goals, we can accidentally end up trading in our personal integrity for the approval and security that a group can engender. Perhaps for the first time in a long time we feel "safe." Riding in the arms, and upon the shoulders of a group, particularly one with a charismatic leader, is not just tempting, it's intoxicating, and no one loves an intoxicant as much as an addict does.

Give egos a place where they can shine anew, in any assembly where hierarchies are firmly in place, where accolade is awarded for homogeneity, and where questioning either doctrine or the sanctity of the group is derided as heresy, and it's like spreading manure in a garden. Sure enough, some stuff will grow under those conditions, but if we get close enough to the ground in such gardens, we'll notice there's a strong odor, too. Thus when choosing teachers and teachings, however lofty, altruistic, and historically correct they might appear, it's our job to not only keep our eyes open, but our noses as well. Paying attention to small inklings can unveil larger stories in such cases. We're back to that bullshit-cutting question, "What do you know that you don't want to know?"

If we examine the nearly ubiquitous black and white yin yang symbol, we notice that it is split into halves, one black and one white. But just as importantly, in most models, there is an "eye" of the opposite color built into each half. The white half has a black eye, and the black half has a white eye. *Within each extremity there lies the seed of the other extremity.* This is the nature of duality, which is, of course, just fine. But this is also a message for *us* that any extremity is never more than a *temporary* position in nature. Drought gives way to flood, storms follow the calm, and day and night replace each other. Nothing stays the same in manifestation, and an extreme position is not an endpoint isolated over to the *side* of life, so much as it is simply another waypoint in the *circle* of life. It will not stand indefinitely.

For spiritual seekers, and perhaps especially for previously *addicted* spiritual seekers, this is a critical point for us to take in. The temptation is always to move from one side of the circle to the other. That's the easiest, most natural move—the common "all or nothing" approach to situations that addicts and, to a lesser degree, all other human beings are so very fond of taking. Such a 180 is not necessarily a bad move. It can be a great move, a giant leap forward. The only problem is that in the long run such choices, when they are defined as the end-point and not another waypoint, will often turn out to be limiting. A spiritual movement that begins in innocence, and with the highest ideals, can all too easily morph into an overall attitude of hubris and condescension. It is the great failing not only of many individuals in any pocket of spirituality, but also of some of the great religious traditions, and they drag along many of their adherents.

The thinking is pretty easy to spot. "I once had no idea what was right, but now I not only know what's right for me, I know what's right for *everybody*." It's a divisional 180 shift, and thus no more than half the available truth.

There is a certain type of person who loves this kind of life in the ranks. They like hard, sharp lines and they learn how to function within them. They learn how to prosper, how to rise within the ranks, and perhaps even how to foster something of a following. When you're working with an entire crowd who's lost and searching, which spiritual organizations typically are, truth can easily become "whatever we say it is." Everybody likes a place to hang their hat in this life, and there's no place more full of hat pegs as spiritual traditions. The world at this level is cleanly and clearly divided up into believers and unbelievers. A macho attitude develops and, "I'm more fundamental than you are" reigns. One only has to read the newspapers, or look at one's own experience, to verify the validity of my observations.

I've played devil's advocate here for the sake of discussion. The fact is that most spiritual groups are overwhelmingly positive and beneficial. They do a lot of good, and they help a lot of people. Allegiance to a group or teacher is just fine—when it is. Our question is ever the same: "Is it right for me—*right now*?"

We've looked at integrity from several angles now. It and earnestness are the left and right hand-pillars of both enlightenment and embodiment. We will do well to cultivate both.

CHAPTER ELEVEN
Step Eleven

ABIDANCE

THE WORDING OF RECOVERY'S 11TH STEP STATES THAT WE ARE BY THIS point seeking to improve conscious contact with our Higher Power, and are now praying "only for his will for us and the power to carry that out." If we are living from the duality of me-God-world, then that last part is a *really* tall order.

Both recovery and Nonduality assume we have attained a certain level of spiritual maturity by the time we hit this step, and the intent of both approaches is essentially the same: pressing forward by living what we have learned. So here there is firm agreement. While the differences may at first appear to be only about semantics, language, however, is a *very* big deal, so we don't want to overlook or dismiss anything in our investigation.

It could be said that Nonduality is fundamentally a very sharp and skillful *languaging* about the nature of ultimate reality. Some would argue, me among them, that it is at least one of, and perhaps *the* most direct way possible (excepting silence) for the divine, for the one thing going on, to talk *to* itself *about* itself *through* itself while it's pretending to be the form of a human being. Let us not underrate the power in linguistics. They can be lights of, for, and by consciousness.

When one is not originating from duality, such as our view here, there is no "we" who needs knowledge of "another's" will.

There is just one thing going on. So regardless of whether the so-called "other" is divine or not, anytime we're dealing with an "other," we've got at least *two* things, and here we are exclusively dealing with *not-two*. Philosophical duality is just fine, and for most people in most situations it's the easiest way of dealing with the world and of approaching spirituality. Within the recovery community, it's bedrock, and should be. I offer no argument with it whatsoever. It worked for me; shall I now throw stones? Duality is not our enemy. Duality, like everything else, is *part of* the great singularity, part of the one thing going on. We will find it quite helpful, however, to learn to *recognize* duality *as* duality. As we have already observed, the chief avenue for discovering what we are is through discovering what we not. So, even if it's merely reminding ourselves over and and over again about our true nature, and our true situation, it's important to do so. Repetition breeds understanding.

In either tradition, however, at this stage we are no longer in the spiritual emergency room. Rather, we are in the spiritual classroom, so to speak, and every one of us is a student, including those at the front of the room who look like teachers. What worked for us yesterday is what worked for us yesterday. If it does not sustain us today, and nothing will do that forever, then let's see if we can open up and find something that does so, without passing a fool's judgment on the sound and helpful tools we're putting down. We put them down with care so that the people behind us can find them and use them. Good tools are not always easy to find.

From the Nondual perspective, we don't need the power to carry out God's will. What we need is the humility to see that we *already are* God's will, that we're *sitting right in the middle* of that will, that *what's going on* is that will, and that there is not, in fact, anything *other than* that will. What's happening is what's happening. However, we comment on it, divide it up, discuss it and dissect it, and it's when we *relate to* what's happening in this way, instead of watching and flowing *as* what's happening, that problems arise. We can only "relate to" what is seen or felt from a center, from a personality, from an imaginary construct that is superimposed upon reality. In short, we can only relate *from* a "me."

Let us clearly understand that when we say, "Thy will be done," we're not giving the universe *permission* to carry on as it wishes. It's *already* doing so, has *always* done so, and always *will* do so (always *in* and *as* the now), with or without our apparent presence, and with or without our make-believe permission. When within Nonduality we say, "Thy will be done," if we say it at all, then we're saying it as a succinct statement about the very *nature* of reality. There is just *one* active will. We call it life. Our job—our *perceived* job, our *apparent* job, as an *apparent* other—is simply to fall into line with that single will. It is our job to step out of the *way* of life, and into the *flow* of it. The title of one of the oldest spiritual books we have, the *Tao Te Ching* translates as "The Way of Life." And it teaches what is always taught in these circles: "A Higher Power's will is always and already being done, whether you like it or not, and you are a holistic part of it, so you might as well get the hell out of the way rather than resist." Life is going to sweep us along *anyway*. You are welcome to stand against it, but it's simply going to run you over if you do. So the only real question is, How much do we want to suffer while the one thing going on *happens*?

The "act of surrender" is never an *actual* surrender. That's just how we speak of it. Here's what I mean. My left hand is "surrendered" to the total action of my body, but it doesn't know it. That's just the way of it. My left hand didn't have to study up on how to surrender, or become surrendered. *It always was already so*, it just didn't consciously know it. My left hand doesn't have to figure out what the body's will is, and what's the best way to follow it. *It is shown, not told.* My left hand picks up a pen, buttons my shirt, or pets the cats without opinion or interference. It doesn't accomplish this by adopting new philosophies or practices to replace what it now considers to be its old and worn philosophies and practices. *It simply never takes on any of those things to begin with.* My left hand is an "empty" tool for this body, as this body is an empty tool for consciousness. My left hand does what it does. It doesn't ask for applause, or a crown, or a gold star, when it does an especially fine job of something. If I stick a ring on one of its fingers, it doesn't get all puffed up about itself. When it's offered food or rest, it takes them. It neither boasts, nor complains. It does what it's supposed to do, or at the very least it does its best.

All of this happens so smooth and slick because my left hand doesn't erroneously think of itself as being a separate entity. It operates as an integral part of an all-encompassing whole, not as something *apart from* an imaginary, threatening "other." I call it "empty," because it is empty of its own identity. It exists only as part of a whole. Any sense of individual identity would have to be *imagined*; it would never be the real case. We are as empty of individual identity as our hands are.

Suppose it was another way. Suppose for a moment that my left hand imagined it was a thing unto itself. Suppose next that it decided it wanted to be the hand-in-charge, instead of the lowly secondary hand, given that I'm naturally right-handed. It might feel sorry for itself. It might bemoan its cruel fate. Would anything change, other than the "mental state" of my left hand? If it thought itself a separate entity, then when I slipped a ring on its finger it might tell a story like, "Well, there, finally, he's seen the obvious: *I'm* the special hand after all! Look! He's put a gold band on my second finger—oh, I see, my God, he's *marrying* me! Yes! Yes! I *am* the chosen one!"

Again, other than what was happening inside the hypothetical "brain" of that hand, would anything be any different? It's all just story, totally made up, cooked up, and totally happening within that thumbnail brain and nowhere else.

Let's refer again to our friend the photographer. If he or she took a picture of you when your mind was going crazy, all the photo would show is your body. The going crazy thing is happening in your head. It's not actually real. There'd be a photo of a person sitting in a chair, perhaps with a turned down mouth. That's all it would show, because that's all that's actually going on *on-planet*. This particular story of "special hand" couldn't be seen or heard by anyone *other than* my left hand, and the story has zero bearing *on* reality, because it in itself *has no* reality.

It would only be a matter of time before my left hand would notice that my right hand was still getting most of the attention. It would take it personally, and now tell the story of how our make-believe "hand in marriage" must not be so meaningful after all; of how it's being taken for granted; of how it's being treated poorly, undervalued and overlooked. Poor, pitiful *me*. Once again it would become restless, irritable, and discontented, and hence less useful and productive. And on and on and on.

The acid test of whether something is real or not is this: reality is something that remains even when it's not thought about. In the situation from above, your body and your table would remain even if you didn't think about them. How about "you"? Your identification with that body disappears as soon as you quit thinking about it, does it not? "You" disappear between every thought. Reincarnation? It's happening thousands of times a day! We have to restart it every morning, because it's been gone for eight hours and we have to reintroduce it to its situation. What isn't real can never be. What is real can never *not* be. When you move all of the objects out of a room, what remains? When all of the thoughts in a mind disappear, what's left? In both cases it's apparently empty space. It is within this apparently empty spaciousness that the whole play of the universe takes place. It's all just *happening*, and it's happening inside of you, not outside of you.

I used "inside" and "outside" conditionally. The happening *is* you; there's no actual inside or an outside of *what is*, but it may be helpful to think that way for a while. We use these metaphors like we use training wheels. They're great while we need them, but there's no point in hanging onto them afterward. They're not trophies; once again they are tools we no longer need.

In a similar way, when we say "surrender," that's another way of saying that we're simply seeing things as they are. We're not in control. We've never been in control, and control is not about to happen. It can't. There's *no one here* to be in control. The whole idea of it is a moot one, a nonsense children's tale. Philosophers have been asking if *we* have free will or not for millennia. My question is more basic. "*Who* in the hell are they talking about?" What does not exist can neither have free will, nor *not* have free will. That discussion is a classic example of how duality keeps us hypnotized by creating and constantly shoring up two severely oppositional sides of a fundamentally nonsensical question.

Now let's take a look at "conscious contact." If while in recovery people begin to sense the presence of something larger than their "little me," that's wonderful. It's the beginning of the end for ego, but it may take a long, long time for that end to come. Lifetimes, maybe, but nonetheless the scene is set and enlightenment is a foregone conclusion.

Many in recovery may find it disturbing when I say that, from the viewpoint of Nonduality, this pursuit is a waste of time. I don't mean that from the standpoint of recovery. These paths are similar, but that's a long way from saying they are interchangeable. I don't recommend Nonduality for getting people clean and sober and abstinent, and I don't recommend recovery as the best path to awakening. Each does what it does very well; let's respect both. I never discovered anything of significance when I was loaded beyond the fact that I always wanted more of whatever the hell it was that I was using to get a state change. The disease of "more," they sometimes call it. I say it's closer to "more *now*." Addiction is a closed, self-affirming system. But recovery can become something of a closed system as well; it's quite circular. That's not a criticism, it's an observation. Addiction and recovery are yin and yang, two sides of the very same coin. Our goal here is to move our view beyond all opposites, including those two.

Once we have seen our true nature, there is no further talk of attempting to *make* or maintain contact with a Higher Power. It's clearly seen that there is no way to *avoid* contact! Contact, in fact, is just not the right word for us. Conscious *current* recognition—dwelling with the knowing, which some call *abidance*—is more accurate. We hear this word tossed about a bit in Nonduality these days, but I'm not at all sure that the way I mean it here is the way it's generally translated elsewhere, so let's start all over with a fresh look. As ever, I'll use a story to help illustrate my point.

I had lunch yesterday with an expatriate American who lives in New Zealand. She knew me from the internet and wanted to get together while she was visiting the States. She was a very pleasant, but rather desperate character. Ah, the gift of desperation! This is someone who'd been searching for conscious contact with a Higher Power for thirty years—she'd sought it all over the world. She hadn't made this envisioned "conscious contact" in America, or India, or Down Under. She told me when we met that she felt like she was "getting ripe." In other words, she had a built-in story of a future that guaranteed she would never satisfy her longing. If we put her search under a microscope, we would see that my friend was looking for something "a little bit *elsewhere*, and just a tad *later*." She was also looking for something objective, essentially a *noun* of some sort, however wispy and vague, with which to make this conscious contact.

We can search not just planet Earth for God, but a thousand other planets, and if we are searching for anything that is anywhere other than right here, at anytime other than right now, our search will by definition be unsuccessful. We lost as soon as we decided to look. If we search for anything objective, we will come up empty-handed. Keeping to that criteria is every bit as hypnotically misleading as the free will argument we just talked about. It is, as Shakespeare said, "Much ado about nothing."

My friend and I sat in a cafe, where I asked some questions, pointed a few things out, and led her through some simple exercises. About an hour into our lunch my friend came to know her true nature. I was still talking (as I am wont to do) when she grabbed my hand and began to cry. I looked in her eyes, and saw that she *knew*. She cried first, and then she began to laugh. We both laughed, because the jig was up, the joke was over, and the punch-line had been revealed. Once the truth is seen, the craziness of our search becomes completely apparent and one simply cannot *not* laugh!

That's because the first step, the very, very first step in any hunt for any Higher Power, is a step *away* from that Higher Power. She didn't have to leave the restaurant in order to have a successful search. She didn't have to wait until later. And she never found anything objective.

God is always *the thing that is looking*. It is always looking here and now, and I remind you that it's not a noun, it's more like a verb. Be*ing*. See*ing*. Know*ing*.

These truths are not merely cold facts that applied in Fred's case, or my friend's case. This applies to *your* case, too, right here and now. The attentiveness reading *this* sentence? God. Awareness. Reality. Being. Our body-minds are sensing devices. The information comes *through* the body-mind, but it isn't just going *to* the body-mind for the benefit of the body-mind. My fingertips send me information through my left hand, but they don't send it to the left hand for the *benefit* of the left hand. My hand is just a pass-through device through which the information is carried. The body is as much like an electrical junction box as anything else. It is also exactly as autonomous as an electrical junction box. The body is mobile and a junction box is not; that's the chief difference between the two. A junction box appears to deliver energy, and the body pretends to think. When a body-mind believes that it is alive and an electrical junction box is not alive, then the junction box is proven to be the wiser of the two. The junction box may not be *right*, but at least it's not *wrong*.

Everything is alive, because everything is life itself. Life itself has no opposite. Birth and death are opposites and extremes *within the dream*, but there is no opposite to life. From the absolute view, nothing is ever born, and certainly nothing ever dies, because beyond the one thing going on, what is there? Nothing. There is *only* the one thing going on, and it *is*. It cannot *not* be. It existed before there was a universe, and it will exist after the universe winks out. *It is existence itself.* And you are it. I am it. Each of us can, with perfect accuracy, state that we are it. Not any *ego*; of course; I don't mean that. You know what I mean. *Big you,* so to speak.

If you are going to look for God, fine; turn your internal gaze around, move that seeking attention *inward*. Don't bother looking elsewhere; it's nowhere else. *Look for what's looking.* Don't even look for it; just notice it, recognize it, acknowledge it. Remember the inquiry called 'Where's Fred?' We looked and looked and looked, but we never looked at the looker; we never paid attention to the *looking itself*, to the *verbness*. Do so now. Really look. Where lives the looker? What *are* you? What are you *really*? Hang there in the unknowing.

There's nothing objective for you to find, is there? But still, there's *something* doing the looking, even if that something is more like nothing than it is a thing. It's not nothing, because it's clearly alive. It's unimaginably intelligent. It's not in your head; it *contains* your head. Yet it's not outside of your head, because when it's seen that there is just one thing going on, inside and outside no longer apply. Where is the inside of space? Where is the outside? Where are the edges to your sense of being? If you've been looking for God, then chances are you've been looking for the same "noun-ness" that my friend and I were looking for. I say again, the one thing going on is a *verb*, a verb that is simultaneously no-thing and every-thing.

God is the very verbness that's looking for itself, but it's been looking in the mirror instead of for *what's casting the reflection*. We've been busily hunting for something objective; but the one thing going on—awareness, let's call it—is not an object. It's exactly the opposite; our body-minds are among the multifarious objects that populate the larger object—our world—but *the single subject to all of those objects*, and all objects everywhere, is *awareness itself*. Look around; *Godness* is happening all around you. Look *at* you; Godness is happening *as* you; or as the you-ness you think you are.

Please see: there is just one thing going on.

It may be helpful initially to think of awareness as being *behind* you. That's fine as a starting place; even a faltering, intellectual grasp of what I'm speaking about can become the small tool that brings down a mountain.

In the presence of a moment of grace, then what my new, New Zealander friend lovingly calls the Gift begins to become open to the truth that consciousness is *not* contained in that body-mind you *think* you are, nor is it outside of it. It is seen that your body-mind is instead contained *within* the consciousness that you *really* are. There are plenty of methods, inquiries and teachers who can help you move from the intellectual position to the living position, if you are so motivated. I don't subscribe to the idea we often hear that a living teacher is necessary to walk through the Gateless Gate, because my own experience proves otherwise, and my own experience is always my benchmark. But a teacher can be damn helpful, let me be clear on that. And they are *at least* as helpful after a true seeing as they are in assisting us experience such a thing. "Waking up" happens out of time. We refer to it as an event, but that's just language. It's not really an event; it's always already here. But "awakening" is usually an apparent event, and always an apparent process, make no mistake about it. Having a guide through that process has been extremely helpful to *me*.

There is another teacher I want to bring up in this chapter, and it's one that we can access immediately, without any more of a spiritual experience than we're already having; without any mystical seeing. That guide is what many call our inner teacher. This is the ever-present guide of all of us on the apparent spiritual journey. Some of us listen to it, and some of us don't. Very few of us listen to it all the time, myself included. It never speaks loudly, but only in whispers. It doesn't offer us any explanation, or justification, and it doesn't hang around to say, "I told you so," if we fail to take its advice. It just whispers and moves on. There is no past or future for our inner teacher. It always arises spontaneously, in the here and now, about the here and now.

If we begin to pay attention to this guide, we tend to get better at hearing it. It doesn't speak any louder, but our ears get more sensitive. I can't know how it works for everyone, but in my case the more I utilize the pointers I receive, "He who has ears to hear, let him hear." I should say here that I'm speaking of an inner voice, but it's probably not going to be *audible*. It's more feeling than voice, but "voice" is a good translation. This voice is with you right now, on the apparent relative plain, regardless of whether you have experienced any so-called awakening or not.

Our inner teacher is quite a practical "being." It pushes me to go to the trouble to hand-wash the plastic peanut butter container instead of throwing it in the trash. It has me put feeding the birds on the top of my list when I'm really busy with self-important stuff. It points out that our pets have as much right to sit in the doorway as I do to walk through it. At other times it sends me insights—almost like downloads. I used to describe it as "The Explainer," which made more than one spiritual teacher laugh knowingly. These insights may be directly linked, or may not be even marginally connected to what's going on at the time. I've had them occur in meditation, but more often in crossing a parking lot, or trimming a hedge. But whenever that advice or information arrives, it always does so as the *truth*. There's never a question about debating it, batting it around in my head, or going to see if some other teacher has something to say about it. The question is, "Will I follow it?" Often yes, but sometimes no. I still have a bit of suffering to do just yet, but thankfully not a lot.

My inner teacher wrote most of this book. I can type quite fast, yet there were many times when I just couldn't type *fast enough*. I don't mean any sort of channeling, or automatic writing. It didn't whisper in my ear in any sort of vocal way, or take my hand in a ghostly embrace. If I heard much in the way of voices, or felt a ghostly embrace, I'd be heading to a psychiatrist. But very often, really *most* of the time during the writing of this, the stories of time and space and personality collapsed and there was *just* typing. There was no one here to "channel" in the conventional sense, but certainly the body-mind was no more than a handy writing tool for consciousness. I was pretty much a giant pencil. My chief job, at least as it has felt to me, has been to keep some sense of momentum going *in between* those runs. So I would fuss for five days over five pages and then write twenty in an afternoon. It never asked if that was the way I wanted to do it. There was no one here for it to question, and no one here to answer.

Our inner teacher helps us operate from our own experience and not the hearsay of the internet, books, or other media. We want to become Buddhas, not *parrots*. So often on the Web I see blogs or comments written by seekers who are busily dispensing advice they themselves have not yet taken. They point out that everything is you, or it, or what have you, all this without having first recognized their own identity. I know of no better way to slam an inner teacher to the mat and make it go quiet. Just act as if you already know something, and it won't bother to suggest otherwise. There's no open space for it to operate, and it will not operate in the face of resistance. A knowing attitude operating out of no-nothingness is resistance of the most base sort. This is one reason why humility is the very foundation of true spiritual progress. Not one-time humility, not yesterday's humility, not I-remember-when-I-had-my-spiritual-awakening humility. This quality, like enlightenment, is now or never; here or nowhere. A *history* of humility is precisely as valuable as some stinking drunk's history of a run of previous sobriety. It might be a pleasant story, but what's it got to do with what's going on now?

Among other things it does, our inner teacher gives us pointers for seemingly integrating the wisdom of the teachings into the dream, after which the dream becomes more and more lucid, and the lines between illusions and reality are seen to be only conceptual. It's a confusing subject that's seemingly within the reach of imagination, but it's actually quite beyond the mind's grasp. I don't know that I could explain it any better than I have—poor as that might be—if I wrote about it for another month. Rather than potentially wasting my time or yours, let me instead mention how to find out about it for yourself. After all, the only thing that matters *to* you is what works *for* you. Everything else is empty information, like selling points on a travel brochure for a trip you're not going to take.

Our inner teacher is always already here. We don't need to *invent* it; we only need to *invite* it. Given that an inner teacher is so quiet and subtle, what would you imagine is most needed to coax it into presenting itself more openly? It needs to have on "this side" what it is coming from on "that side:" silence and stillness. Like begets like. Our inner teacher is not a separate, spooky entity; it's sort of a bridge between the worlds, the connection that links the relative and the absolute. Of course, it's actually communicating with itself, but speaking here from an absolute view won't be very helpful to us, so let's stick to the relative viewpoint.

I'm suggesting a practice here. Do it if you're drawn to it. I've already stated that I think practices have their place, and this is one of those places. We really just do them to do them. In a devotion-based religion or philosophy we would say that we do our practice out of love—for our god, our guru, or some such entity—at least a conceptual "other," even if the overall understanding ends up being Nondual. Well, we can still do our meditation out of devotion, but here let's do it out of a love of *truth*. Let us go to the very wellspring of truth, to the source of truth itself. Let us take a journey without distance to our source, the source of our very lives, the source of the universe itself, and allow the unknown truth to unveil itself to itself.

Of course we won't bother to pretend that we won't have the subtle goal of either encouraging or expanding awakeness. I wanted to awaken more than anything else, and I think that's a large part of why I apparently did. But for this sitting, let's allow that desire to be a goal-less goal; something that perhaps can't fail to be there, but which we pay as little attention to as possible, at least for the length of this practice. The practice I'm suggesting here is meditation, but it's meditation with a little bit of a twist. This certainly didn't originate from me. It didn't originate from anybody. I can say that it's helpful.

Exercise 9: Meditation and the Inner Teacher

*

Unless we already have sitting cushions that we're surpassingly comfortable with, let's just use a chair; any chair, a *comfortable* chair, no less. Let's not make this goal-less sitting into some sort of ritual. Let's not put on any music, or light up any incense, or put on special clothes. Let's not ferociously take on any special postures, or adopt any secret handshakes. Instead, let's just look normal—for us, and act normal—for us. Let's sit in a relaxed manner, in our own home, in our own chair, in regular clothes, in a comfortable sitting position, not necessarily slouched, but not ramrod straight either. We're not trying to be mystical, or holy, or Eastern. We're not trying to be anything. We're just exactly who we are, as we are, sitting still with our eyes closed; nothing to it.

All we want to do is simply to be as quiet and still as we can, thus opening up a "vacancy," if you will. We are not *creating* space, but we are *allowing* some spaciousness to clear if it wants to. We're also allowing it to stay loaded up with thoughts if it wants to! If we come back to this sitting often enough, then most of the time the body-mind will receive the preparatory signals and look forward to relaxing. As they say, it takes what it takes until it takes. We're simply allowing everything to be as it is anyway, *especially* our minds. I do this almost every day for ten minutes to thirty minutes. Even five minutes is a lot better than no minutes. Do what you can; don't worry about what you don't do. Sometimes I go through a period where I do this twice a day, but I notice that doesn't usually last for long. Twenty minutes would be my average. I just sit. When my twenty-pound Maine Coon comes and crawls in my lap, that's fine as well. I sit quietly, but alertly, and he naps. We are both being ourselves. If someone cranks up a weed-eater next door, okay, that's fine. It's part of what's happening; it's not breaking anything up, it's *part of* it. The furnace or air conditioning cycles; the refrigerator clucks out its little noises. It all just *is*. There's a perfect *suchness* to each moment.

And then the harp music on my iPhone goes off. I open my eyes, pet the cat, indicate I'm rising, and off we go, headed upstairs to the office to begin our day's work. Generally speaking, nothing unusual will have happened. No mystic visions. No great insight. No cramps, either! No look-at-me-the-mystic sort of headiness or glory. Just sitting; nothing special.

When I arrive in my office upstairs, everything in the room is just like it was downstairs: it *is*. It's a nice room, but it's not *my* room. Computer, books, lamp, photos. Lovely filtered light. There is *suchness* upstairs, too. I take my place at the computer. Just sitting; nothing special.

This simple little everyday *no-practice-practice* might very well help change your world if you adopt it in conjunction with some of the teaching we've discussed. That quiet, still time seems to create enough vacancy for something new to happen, for movement to occur, and that something new usually comes through our inner teacher. We begin to hear from it, or we begin to be moved by it, however one would wish to put it. Whispers come. If we don't listen, it'll retire again until it's once again either encouraged, or desperately needed. I can look at several serious traffic accidents that never happened, because something took over the car for me. I know what that was, and where it came from. There wasn't time even to *ask* for help, help just *came*. I can look at the source of the vast bulk of whatever apparent spiritual progress has been made here, and know it's through the very same medium. I did not call it teacher during those dangerous moments, but it is the same thing speaking in another way.

Let's recall the make-up of our true nature for a moment. We've talked about this before. What is it that consciousness does? It *welcomes*. It welcomes everything, just as it is. We could say it welcomes everything *when* it is, *where* it is, but of course that's dream talk. There's no time other than now, and no place other than here. In the strictest sense of things, there is not even anything to welcome! But for now we'll say that this here and now is composed *of* consciousness, exists *within* consciousness, and is witnessed *by* consciousness. So when we sit quietly, resisting nothing, allowing everything, we are actually practicing *being ourselves*, or our *oneself*, if you will. That's what true meditation, as it is sometimes called, means. We our practicing being what we really are, which is quite a large change from identifying exclusively and often miserably with one little speck of a human body among all the universes! That's such a limited and limiting view.

Because of my checkered past, when some kind or loving action comes through this body, I am often quietly amazed. I'm no longer *surprised* at it, but I am still quietly amazed. I don't take this change for granted; it's wonderful and magical. How could that have happened? How could such a dramatic shifting possibly be taking place here, so that kindness and love would automatically emanate? Through grace. It's all grace. This meditation I'm speaking of, this quiet sitting, could be said to be one of the ways I continue to *court* grace, and to *thank* grace, although grace neither requires, nor responds to my gratitude. But I do.

I don't try to figure all of this out, to pigeon-hole it in any way. Certainly *something* is working, and this change is not hit or miss, it's broad based and it broadens yet more every day. It's reminiscent of the early days of getting clean and sober. Other people could see a revolution of evolution occurring before I could. They shared their thoughts, and I sometimes wondered who they' were talking about. This can be like that as well.

Another similar meditation practice is to simply stop and relax into space, into our sense of being, as we go about our day, many times a day. We just pause and notice awareness. Just notice that everything is always already present. We don't have to do a thing to create it. We don't have to take measures to combat it, or adjust it. From the larger view, we've already accepted it; it's pointless to turn around and resist it. If we so choose, we can just relax and actually *be* it. A few seconds is all it takes. We can do this when we're working, when we're eating, mowing the lawn, or walking to the mailbox.

It's another nice little no-practice-practice that's easy, instantly pleasing, and fruitful if pursued. Try it if you like. You could even try *both* types if you wanted to. You would try them both not by *doing* anything, but by devoting apparent time to *being* everything. It's quite a switch, but it can really move us a long way in a relatively short period of apparent time. Even relative shifting is still positive movement, and everyone we deal with will appreciate it as much or more than we do.

Through meditation we can come to a place where we never fail to know who we really are. This security is enormously freeing. It's actually the only security there is: the total lack of security. How did the song go, many years ago? "Freedom's just another word for nothing left to lose." Weird, huh? We may not always behave in accordance with that knowledge, but if we "keep coming back," as they say in the rooms, then slowly but surely we lose more and more, and as we do, more of our behavior will fall into line with our new knowing, which we could call not-knowing! Compulsive thoughts begin to fall away. Seeking drops entirely. If we keep coming back to the place of unknowing, eventually the apparent pendulum swings of present/not present, awake/asleep can end for us as well. And simultaneously we get to let everyone else off the wheel of the awake/asleep trap. How? By asking, *What everybody else*? There is just one thing going on. We come to consciously, knowingly abide in that one thing.

I now invite you to take the next step, which is always the one right in front of you. It is, of course, both our last step and our first.

CHAPTER TWELVE
Step Twelve

PRACTICE

IN THE RECOVERY TRADITION, THIS IS WHERE WE VOW TO SHARE WHAT we've learned with suffering addicts, and practice the principles of the steps in all our affairs. The Nondual community has no policy or mission statement about *anything*, including transmission, but history shows us that upon awakening a natural movement for some is to teach. The efficiency and effectiveness of spreading the opportunities of each tradition have been multiplied many times over by sweeping changes in their landscapes. As with all news it's mixed, but I think the overall pattern is positive. Let's take a look at what I mean.

One of the finer ideas in recovery's Twelve Traditions, among many fine ideas, is that the fellowship is to share, and thereby increase, membership through a program of "attraction, not promotion." I like that stance very much. The fellowships do present themselves to potential members via strategically placed pamphlets, liaisons with the professional community, listings in the phone book and online, and meetings in treatment centers, but suffice it to say none of us have ever seen a TV ad for a recovery fellowship.

The recovery community has the luxury of this approach due to the fact that "twelve step work," as working with other addicts is called, is done purely as an avocation. (Fellowship members do work in treatment centers, but it's not considered part of their twelve step work.) Recovery teachings say that sharing is beneficial to the sharer, because it helps keep them sober. In fact, it is seen as the primary and most effective vehicle of maintaining sobriety. There's nothing that makes one more clear about one's own addiction condition than having someone actively suffering from the same condition right in front of one's nose. It worked for me.

However, the landscape has changed dramatically in the last few decades. There are private and public treatment centers and halfway houses, which I think can be very valuable. Treatment centers dominate the stages of treatment where the addict is still-reeking, so to speak. A few weeks later, they often release patients into halfway houses, which vary widely in their approach and effectiveness. A lot of them turn a tidy profit from helping addicts get reestablished in the community. I'm not saying that's wrong, I'm just saying it's not the way things once were.

A great number of treatment centers, I suspect the majority, offer Twelve Step-based programs, and they charge money as well—a *lot* of money. Many of them run TV ads and put up billboards. Again, I'm not criticizing this; I'm just reporting it. Thus while no fellowship casts itself in the spotlight, Twelve Step recovery *does* have media ads of a sort, but they are run *for* it by *proxy*. While treatment centers and halfway houses are sometimes spoken of disparagingly in recovery circles, they do provide a vital service. The old way of non-professional treatment, and of bringing newcomers into our homes simply isn't practiced any longer, or at least it is quite rare.

I know, because I lived early AA through my father. He joined AA in the forties, and when I came along in the fifties, we had an alcoholic living in our spare bedroom upstairs for most of my childhood. There had been one there ever since my oldest brother left home, years before I knew what was going on. I also saw him crawl out of bed and drive into the night on rescue missions over and over again—and then go to work the next day. He picked up one chip and never took a drink before he died forty years later.

Nonprofessional, we're-all-in-the-trenches-together recovery *community* was the way it worked fifty, sixty, seventy years ago.

Recovery today is almost unrecognizable from what I witnessed as a child. And although today's methods are certainly the easiest way to handle a burgeoning community of addicts, the numbers indicate today's methods may not be as effective. There's never a zig without a zag, or a yin without a yang.

The Nondual tradition has grown in quite a different way. There are plenty of groups, but no central core. The circumstances are wildly different, of course, so there is no equivalent to either the central government of the fellowships, or the proxy support of the treatment/halfway house community. Nondual organizations usually are built around a particular teacher or teaching. Where the two traditions are similar is in their grass roots meetings. The message of either teaching is still best delivered face to face. It's not absolutely necessary in either case, but it's very helpful in both. I can't express how grateful I am to the teachers who've been so kind and generous as to work with me. My God, the patience they've shown!

Nonduality has exploded in the last decade or so due to two events. One is the internet and the other, which I imagine will make some people groan, is the publication of *The Power of Now*. Love it, or less-than-love-it, *The Power of Now* was a seminal book in building the groundswell of contemporary Nonduality. It was that book's author, Eckhart Tolle, who led me from Zen to Advaita. As ever, I did everything backward and went from Z to A! When I first heard of Tolle, back in 2002, I couldn't find a copy of his book in this city. Since then he's risen to rock-star status, pals around with movie stars, and has Oprah's private number. She and Tolle did a ten-week online "course" in 2008 that had as many as *two million* people watching it at a shot.

That sort of big time Hollywood-style event had a lot of us feeling very itchy—me among them, I confess. Such a giant, lit-up show of what is an overall subtle, deeply intimate teaching is fraught with potential problems. Yet it did bring a lot of attention to an alternative way of looking at the world, one that surely breeds lighter planetary footprints, so overall it was a great service that no one *but* Oprah could have provided. I'm grateful to her for having the willingness to use her resources the way she did. She took some hits from the conservative crowd, but it'll take more than a few slings and arrows to bring down the great bird that is Oprah Winfrey, Inc. It's so easy to criticize the people who are out front *doing*. I try to ask *what I'm doing in comparison* before I throw too many stones. It's a lot easier to tear down than it is to build up.

The internet has been the greatest message-carrier of Nonduality in its multi-millennial history. The field seems to be mushrooming as a result of this incredible new tool of communication, and I don't see any end to it. From where I sit it looks like the "spiritual quickening" that I spoke of in the introduction is well underway and gaining momentum. Never before has it been so easy for so few to reach so many. And it's so *fast*. I saw my own little blog burst from a tiny following to one with thousands of readers in a matter of months.

The yang side of the internet's dramatic helpfulness has been that the quality of the teachings available runs the full gamut—from the sublime to the ridiculous. One has to hope that the majority of spiritual seekers are wiser than some of the bloggers and YouTubers out there. I suspect they are. And ultimately I have great faith that it's all going just as it should, because it *can't not* go just as it should. Some will wake up and some will sleep soundly—at least until they don't. It's no different than the way it's always been, except that what's happening now is occurring much faster and on a far grander scale.

And of course the relative stakes are much higher as well. Either the planet is going to make a giant turnaround or we humans may have to face going the way of dinosaurs. It's going to take something either completely disastrous, or completely fabulous—or both—to bring about such a radical change. All we can do is *watch*, of course, but while we're watching we can allow our characters all the leeway we can to do their utmost to *be the change*.

Let's now turn away from the macro view of things and move toward the micro.

Once a teacher has apparently made the decision to devote herself or himself to teaching full time, then there are practical matters they have to deal with to insure that they and their family survive the shift. This means charging money for experience, expertise, and services rendered, whether it's a book, or an hour of dialoguing. In no other field would this cause anyone to shudder. It doesn't make me shudder in this one. I have no problem whatsoever with mixing spirituality and commerce. Fundamentally, one is not any more or less "spiritual" than the other. In our world commerce is often the most efficient way for change to happen, to get things done. More real change can happen faster this way than any other of which I'm aware. I don't think our planet has the luxury to wait out our being noble and holy while our habitat collapses under the weight of unconscious motivations and behaviors.

Granted, if the world shakes off human life, from the absolute view there's no problem. We may, however, have a tough time explaining that to our children. It is indeed the meek who shall inherit the earth—our babies, and our babies' babies. Without a vast internal change, what they end up with won't be anything to brag about. So, in the spirit of adventure, let's smile and pay a few dollars if we have the wonderful opportunity to either attend Nondual meetings, or to talk to a teacher one-on-one on the phone, Skype, or in person. Let's just do it in the same manner we spend a few dollars with Amazon to buy a Nondual book—or *any other* book. It's just business. And it's just okay.

In regard to the individual practitioner, while the two traditions certainly take a different approach to this step, once again the goal remains the same for each: *application*. We move from theory to practice, and make it available to others. At least part of our time is spent venturing away from school and into the world. In recovery we begin to live what we *know*. By that I mean, we have a new structure, a new way of living, and we freely offer to share it. In Nonduality, we begin to live what we *are*, meaning we begin to take our stand as awareness, and start to act from our true nature, even if our understanding is not yet completely grounded. Just like recovery, action can do what words cannot. We move a lot further a lot faster from stepping on unknown ground than we do by wondering where the just-right place to take a step might be.

In either case, we are now in a position to be of greater service to others now, and it's our responsibility to be so. There's nothing personal about either recovering from addiction, or being struck by so-called enlightenment. Neither event is for us, or about us. Nor are the processes that follow those events. There is certainly a body-mind who benefits from both of those things, but it also benefits from rainfall and sunshine, and those aren't about it either.

So in the spirit of keeping the stream flowing and the land healthy, we give up being takers, and take on being givers. Recovery has the tradition of sponsorship and other service roles, as well as the stated movement to "practice these principles in all our affairs." Nonduality's view is probably best stated through the Zen Ox-herding Pictures. Those pictures (which are easily Googled) show ten rather arbitrary stages of the journey to and of enlightenment, from aimless seeking, finding a path, and getting a glimpse, all the way through to full, abiding enlightenment, where we "return to the village" to share not just what we know, but who we are. I'll share what first-hand knowledge I have, once again because it might be useful to others, not because it's anything special.

In my own experience, rather than their being staid zones, I find that the so-called levels represented by the Ten Bulls, as the pictures are also called, form something of a ladder that I tend to climb up and down. Happily, the first few seem to be solidly gained, at least until they're not. Others remain fleeting experiences which still come and go. I'm convinced that my mentors are more stabilized than I am, which also leaves them clearer. Good for them; I'm grateful to have them as mentors. But I don't envy them or anyone else. I'm happy and lucky to be where I am. Life is completely amazing from the time I surrender to the call of the waking world, to the moment I surrender to the peace of the world of sleep, particularly deep sleep. My days, even the less than joyful ones, are spent in wonderment. Each moment, on reflection, can be understood to be perfect. It's not worth your trying to figure that out. Find out for yourself.

If I make apparent progress from here, great, but I can neither force it to happen, nor stop it from happening. It's way too late for that; I'm far past the point of no return—not that I'd ever want to return. We're right back to H.O.W. That's what we can do at this point: remain as honest, open, and willing as we can. This is another way of saying that if we want to be useful, then we should hang around the fire station, smile and serve coffee, but otherwise stay the hell out of the universe's way! Setting or putting out fires is none of our business. Nonetheless, we make this a *test* stop, and not merely a *rest* stop. We test what we know out in the real world.

The final photo of the Zen Ox-herding Pictures is of the wanderer-become-sage coming full circle and returning to the village to help others. Even in the light of awakening—*especially* in the light of awakening—those through whom awakeness is *presently* functioning will find ways to care for their fellow human beings. One doesn't have to be enlightened in order to be inherently useful. Lots of good people do a great deal of fine work from all walks of life and all levels of spiritual understanding. But selfless service is a hallmark of awakeness. There is just one thing going on, and it is always ready and willing to help itself, to comfort itself, to feed and love itself, in the most open-hearted and generous ways.

If you think you are awake, or consider yourself a serious student of spirituality, but you find that your time is generally still tied up stirring your own stew, it might be time to "take an inventory," as the recovery folks would tell us. I know a goodly number of what we would call "enlightened beings" all across America, as well as in Canada, England, and Australia, and every single one of them is making themselves useful right here, right now, on this spinning little planet called Earth, within the relative world, within the dream, yet from beyond the dream. I have heard it said in spiritual circles that who we are is more important than what we do. I don't know enough to debate that. But I do know that if who we are doesn't spill out into what we do, then we are probably *not* who we think we are. *Who we are* is ultimately what we teach.

Who *are* you? Who are you, *really*? Find out and live from there.

Once again, enlightenment is not about us. It's not about us, and it's not *for* us. How do I know this so very certainly? Well, the most obvious tip-off is that there is no "us," not in the final understanding. That wipes the slate absolutely clean. No person is ever asleep. No person ever wakes up. Yet even those who discover their true nature generally forget this, sometimes almost immediately. It becomes "my" awakening, and the "my" as it's used here is not merely a helpful linguistic convention, but is an actual, working belief on their part.

This is rather similar to those in the rooms of recovery who make a point of claiming to be among "the chosen ones." Bull. This simply bolsters the sense of separation. It's still a cry to be special, and can only come at the expense of the *unspecial* ones, the *unblessed* ones. We still remain unwilling to simply be "one of." It's a subtle story to make us feel like we *are* something, or *did* something to deserve what we have. We aren't, we haven't, and we weren't. It just happened, as part of the whole movement of the universe which does not recognize an "us" at all. Nothing happens for the sake of any individual. This leaves us in pure gratitude rather than comparative gratitude.

There's absolutely nothing in either recovery or enlightenment for an individual to claim, or own, or to either get full of themselves, or down on themselves about. All of that may happen anyway; I would guess that in both traditions it usually does, at least for a while. Hopefully we'll grow out of it. In at least Nonduality we want to *see* the movement and then dismiss it as quickly as we can. If we don't clamor for separation, if we want truth more than comfort or accolade, those stories will drop away of their own accord. If we don't, they won't, and they'll serve as the capstone of our spiritual development. That's as far as we go. None of it has anything whatsoever to do with authentic, living enlightenment, or even authentic, living recovery.

There's just one thing going on, and it's right here, right now, working through me, through you, through all of us. The universe is waking up to the fiction it has been spinning for itself for so very long; to the long, strange dream of volition, autonomy, and separation. It's just a *story*. Let us see the handwriting on the wall!

We find our way along the path, and then we find a way to serve, just as water finds its way downhill, and then collects at the bottom, forming a drinking pool. High and low, rich and poor, all drink in the same manner, from the same pool, each according to their inheritance, each according to their foremost desires. The pool keeps itself clean and clear by finding, or creating, inlets and outlets; there is always movement, always *flow*. It serves as source itself, taking on all reflections, yet retaining none of them. It is changeless, yet all change takes place upon it, and apparently within it. It asks for nothing, yet everything comes, and everything goes; no appearance stands forever. It offers a universe—it offers *life itself*—yet takes nothing. It is empty, yet gives birth to the world of the 10,000 things, over and over again.

In the end there is only *poolness*, a still, silent depth; a dark, infinite field of boundless possibilities, forever and ever, amen.

Pass it on.

Visit Fred's websites:

www.awakeningclarity.blogspot.co.uk
www.beyond-recovery.org

ACKNOWLEDGEMENTS

It takes a village to raise a Fred. A great many people have played a role in raising this one. To mention them all would be another book. Allow me to bring at least a few to the fore. My love and gratitude go out to:

Three very wise and amazingly generous spiritual teachers who are also dear friends: Greg Goode, Scott Kiloby, and Rupert Spira, who together have cultivated robust clarity out of some very poor ground. I thank them a second time for contributing their precious time and considerable talent toward making this a better book. Gentlemen, I bow.

The kind and generous friends in the Nondual community who have gone out of their way to make a relative newcomer to the larger scene feel welcome: the great communicator, Chris Hebard; the great umbrella of Nonduality, Jerry Katz; my dear, and oh-so-patient editor, Catherine Noyce, and my prescient, altruistic publisher, Julian Noyce. Again to Greg Goode, who helped tremendously with editing and encouragements.

A few of the compassionate souls who at one time or another saved me from myself: John Delgado, Chester & Betty Hackett, Lynn Hunter Hackett, Tammy Kelly, Charlie N., Lloyd S., and Mike & Peg Wilson.

The followers of this path who've shown love and tolerance in allowing me to grow as a teacher while being in their company: Betsy again, along with Chuck, Iliana, Larry, Mary, Melinda, Mo, Tammy, Vince, the people who've written to me through Awakening Clarity, and all of my friends in Twelve Step fellowships. James Waite, Vicki Woodyard, and Neil Dunlap for their steadfast encouragement.

Thank you, thank you, thank you, one and all. Without all of you, this book would not be what it is, and without *some* of you, the author wouldn't *be* at all.

RECOMMENDED READING

Contemporary Titles on Nonduality

Wake Up Now; Stephan Bodian
Living Reality; James Braha
Consciousness Is All; Peter Francis Dziuban
I Am; Jean Klein
As It Is; Tony Parsons
Presence; Rupert Spira (two volumes)
The New Earth; Eckhart Tolle
Nothing to Grasp; Joan Tollifson

Recovery-specific Nonduality

Natural Rest for Addiction; Scott Kiloby

Titles for Conducting Inquiry

The Direct Path: A User Guide; Greg Goode
Loving What Is; Byron Katie

Daily Meditation Books

A Net of Jewels: Daily Pointers for Seekers of Truth; Ramesh Balsekar
365 Tao: Daily Meditations; Ming-Dao Deng

NOTE: For the sake of brevity, this baker's-dozen list restricts itself to
recommending a single book from each author.

THE TWELVE STEPS OF ALCOHOLICS ANONYMOUS*

1. We admitted we were powerless over alcohol—that our lives had become unmanageable.

2. Came to believe that a Power greater than ourselves could restore us to sanity.

3. Made a decision to turn our will and our lives over to the care of God *as we understood Him*.

4. Made a searching and fearless moral inventory of ourselves.

5. Admitted to God, to ourselves, and to another human being the exact nature of our wrongs.

6. Were entirely ready to have God remove all these defects of character.

7. Humbly asked Him to remove our shortcomings.

8. Made a list of all persons we had harmed, and became willing to make amends to them all.

9. Made direct amends to such people wherever possible, except when to do so would injure them or others.

10. Continued to take personal inventory and when we were wrong promptly admitted it.

11. Sought through prayer and meditation to improve our conscious contact with God, *as we understood Him*, praying only for knowledge of His will for us and the power to carry that out.

12. Having had a spiritual awakening as the result of these Steps, we tried to carry this message to alcoholics, and to practice these principles in all our affairs.

CONSCIOUS.TV

CONSCIOUS.TV is a TV channel which broadcasts on the internet at www.conscious.tv. It also has programmes shown on several satellite and cable channels around the world including the Sky system in the UK where you can watch programmes at 8pm every evening on channel No. 192. Conscious.tv aims to stimulate debate, question, enquire, inform, enlighten, encourage and inspire people in the areas of Consciousness, Non-Duality, Science and Spirtuality. It also has a section called 'Life Stories' with many fascinating interviews. You can also find us on the new Samsung Smart (also known as Connected and Hybrid) TVs where we are under the 'video' section.

There are over 300 interviews to watch including several with communicators on Non-Duality including Adyashanti, Darryl Bailey, David Bingham, Marlies Cocheret, Ellen Emmet, Bob Fergeson, Jeff Foster, Steve Ford, Robert Forman, Suzanne Foxton, Tim Freke, Gangaji, Greg Goode, Tess Hughes, Scott Kiloby, Richard Lang, Francis Lucille, Roger Linden, Wayne Liquorman, Jac O'Keefe, Kenneth Madden, Bentinho Massaro, Mooji, Catherine Noyce, Tony Parsons, Halina Pytlasinska, Genpo Roshi, John De Ruiter, Satyananda, Richard Sylvester, Rupert Spira, Florian Schlosser, Mandi Solk, James Swartz, Art Ticknor, Brad Warner, and Pamela Wilson. There is also an interview with UG Krishnamurti. Some of these interviewees also have books available from Non-Duality Press.

Do check out the channel as we are interested in your feedback and any ideas you may have for future programmes. Email us at info@conscious.tv with your ideas or if you would like to be on either of our email lists. You can be on the 'Newsletter list' (every 3 months) or on our 'New Programme Alert list' which means you will be notified every time a new programme is loaded and also receive the newsletter.

CONVERSATIONS ON NON-DUALITY
Twenty-Six Awakenings

The book explores the nature of true happiness, awakening, enlightenment and the 'Self' to be realised. It features 26 expressions of liberation, each shaped by different life experiences and offering a unique perspective.

The collection explores the different ways 'liberation' happened and 'suffering' ended. Some started with therapy, self-help workshops or read books written by spiritual masters, while others travelled to exotic places and studied with gurus. Others leapt from the despair of addiction to drugs and alcohol to simply waking up unexpectedly to a new reality.

The 26 interviews included in the book are with: David Bingham, Daniel Brown, Sundance Burke, Katie Davis, Peter Fenner, Steve Ford, Jeff Foster, Suzanne Foxton, Gangaji, Richard Lang, Roger Linden, Wayne Liquorman, Francis Lucille, Mooji, Catherine Noyce, Jac O'Keeffe, Tony Parsons, Bernie Prior, Halina Pytlasinska, Genpo Roshi, Florian Schlosser, Mandi Solk, Rupert Spira, James Swartz, Richard Sylvester and Pamela Wilson.

CPSIA information can be obtained at www.ICGtesting.com
Printed in the USA
LVOW11s1341030814

397271LV00001B/243/P